THE SOLUTION SYSTEM

MASTERING CONSCIOUSNESS AND CREATIVITY

DAVID IRA ROTTENBERG

A Cedar Crest Book

ISBN: 978-0-910291-25-5

Library of Congress Control Number: 2022945039

Edited by Christy Cole
ChristyColeEditing@outlook.com

Cover design by Farrukh Bala
Book design by Charlyn_designs

First printing edition 2022

Cedar Crest Books
Natick, MA 01760
USA

To Maharishi

Where love reigns, the impossible may be obtained.

Indian Proverb

Be the change you want in the world.

Ghandi

The brain's fundamental secret will be laid open one day. But even when it has, the wonder will remain, that mere wet stuff can make this bright inward cinema of thought, of sight and sound and touch bound into a vivid illusion of an instantaneous present, with a self, another brightly wrought illusion, hovering like a ghost at its centre. Could it ever be explained, how matter becomes conscious?

Ian Mcewan—Saturday

CONTENTS

ACKNOWLEDGEMENTS

In 1970, I began the Transcendental Meditation® technique. From my first meditation, I found the technique incredibly rewarding. Two years later, I became a teacher of the TM® technique. Since that time, I have spent many, many hours listening to lectures by Maharishi Mahesh Yogi, the founder of the TM® program, in-person and on tape, and spent many, many more hours meditating. Since the 1970's, I've also worked as a writer, and, like many people engaged in that task, pondered the question of where ideas come from. This book is the result of all these experiences. In particular, Maharishi's influence permeates these pages. For a few years in the 1980s, I worked as a producer for Light Video & Television. The CEO of that company was Michael Shane, a visionary entrepreneur. His ideas on information have also influenced my thinking. Any faults in this book are my own.

CHAPTER 1

Problems

AHA!

The word is the universal shout of eureka. The glorious gasp of inspiration. The exultant exclamation of insight.

"Aha" is the flash when two thoughts connect. The spark when an idea strikes. The glow when art and invention unite, and as such, it is a moment that is hallowed, studied, and sought after. Yet, as analyzed and desired as the moment is, it is a moment veiled in mystery.

Like a beautiful woman, a solution often dances just out of reach. A solution seems to exist solely on its own terms without rhyme or reason, and no matter how much it is adored and worshiped, it comes and goes solely as it pleases. No one knows how or why solutions occur. Even the greatest geniuses who are touched most often by its quick bright hands do not know:

> When I am, as it were completely myself, entirely alone, and of good cheer—say, traveling in a carriage, or walking after a good meal, or during the night when I cannot sleep; it is on such occasions that my ideas flow best and most abundantly. *Whence* and *how* they come, I know not; nor can I force them...[1]
> **Wolfgang Amadeus Mozart—Composer**

How are poems made? My instinctive answer is a flat 'I don't know.' It makes not the slightest difference that the question as asked me refers solely to my own poems, for I know as little of how they are made as I do of anyone else's.[2]

Amy Lowell—Poet

I have no idea whence this tide comes, or where it goes, but when it begins to rise in my heart, I know that a story is hovering in the offing.[3]

Dorothy Canfield—Writer

Where the ideas come from, I do not know. I do not seek them, directly or indirectly. I can grasp them in my hands, walking out of doors in the woods, in the middle of the night or in the early morning. A poet translates such moods into words. I turn them into sounds.[4]

Ludwig Van Beethoven—Composer

For some days I had carried the idea about with me continually. At last, *I do not know how,* I found it, together with a large number of curious and new considerations concerning the theory of probability.[5]

Andre Marie Ampere—Physicist/ Mathematician

As the above quotes show, for those of brilliance (and for we of more ordinary talent), the source of ideas remains a mystery. No matter who we are or what our profession, the harder we chase after insights, the farther away they slip. Yet, how is this possible? How can ideas well up in our mind without our knowing their source or how they occur?

Throughout the ages, artists, philosophers, and scientists have sought the answer to this question. They have sought in such diverse and arcane areas as the personality and behavior of geniuses, the structure and operation of the brain, the nature and relationship of thoughts, and in the gathering and organizing of information. Yet, none of these areas have yielded any significant results.

Take, for example, information. Information is a bit of data. A scrap of fact. A morsel of evidence. Any individual pursuing a solution needs to gather and organize as much information as possible. If we're an entrepreneur starting a business, we need to know what kind of product or service we should sell; where and how we should sell it; how much we should charge; how we should advertise it—our list of questions goes on and on. Yet, as we seek our solutions, it is not separate bits and pieces of information that provides us with the answers. It is the *connection* of information, and the connection of information does not take place on a piece of paper or in a computer. The connection of information— the "a*ha*" and "eureka" moment—when separate bits of information combine to form an idea—is an experience that takes place in our head. And when we say our head, we mean more than that part of our anatomy which exists between our ears. If we analyze the specific conditions necessary for solutions, what we realize is that more than just our brain— we need our brain to be awake.

The necessity of wakefulness for solutions might seem an obvious point, but in fact it is often overlooked, ignored or, astonishingly, even deemed unnecessary. However, as we shall see, consciousness, alertness, awareness is the key to solutions.

CHAPTER 2

Consciousness Is the Key to Solutions

Solving problems requires connecting words, colors, notes or numbers in new and original ways. But if we are not awake, we cannot connect anything. If we're half-awake, we can think but not very well. If we're awake but drunk, whatever mental alertness we have is dull and distorted and our thoughts are almost completely unreliable for solving problems. If we're in a dream, thinking perhaps, to some extent, takes place, but again our thoughts are confused, disjointed, and unreliable for effective problem solving. Yes, there are instances when a problem is solved in a dream or a drunken stupor (the reasons for which we'll discuss in Chapter 12), but for now we should understand that these instances only demonstrate that awareness, even when at a minimum, is necessary for solutions. *"Aha"* experiences ALWAYS occur when an individual has some degree of awareness, whether that awareness occurs right after regaining consciousness in the morning, when awakened in the middle of the night, in a dream, or in a drunken stupor. The *"aha"* experience ALWAYS occurs in a state of awareness and is thus a product of consciousness—not sleep, drowsiness, dreams, alcohol, or any other drug. And of all possible mental states for solving problems, by far the most favorable is when we are fully alert because the clearer and wider awake our consciousness is, the better we absorb, analyze, organize, and connect information.

The real basis for solving problems is not our physical brain or the information recorded in it. The real basis for solving problems is our consciousness. More than anything else, *the state of our consciousness dictates how well we solve problems. Without consciousness, without alertness, without wakefulness, without awareness, no solutions occur.*

Personality has little to do with solving problems. Psychologists have long analyzed the personalities of geniuses in the hope of finding some common trait to provide a key to solutions. However, geniuses are shy, outgoing, moody, even-tempered, kind, cold, stingy, generous, angry, and loving. For every genius like Beethoven or Van Gogh who fits the clichéd, romantic concept of the frustrated, brooding artist, there are other happy, gregarious geniuses like Bach, Matisse, or Einstein who do their work, call it a day, and go home. Then, of course, there are geniuses like Mozart and Mendelsohn who perform such prodigious feats of creativity at such young ages that it is hard to ascribe solutions to some aspect of their preteen personality. Personalities change. Personalities vary from individual to individual yet all individuals are, at least, sometimes capable of solutions, and capable of solutions at almost any age. Of course, some people arrive at more solutions than others and some solutions have deeper and more lasting significance, but the ability to arrive at solutions is not exclusive to any one personality type.

Certainly, one personality may result in an individual becoming a mathematician and another personality becoming an artist. As well, personality influences the "tone" of what we create. For instance, a gloomy writer may write gloomy books; a happy writer, happy books. However, these aspects of personality only touch the edges of solutions. Whether we are grumpy, happy, arrogant, childlike, or opinionated, we are not going to solve problems if we are not awake.

True, some personality traits such as curiosity and persistence help in promoting solutions but plenty of people who are curious and persistent struggle with problem-solving. They sit at a desk, sweating for a solution—just like everyone else—and have no idea how or why solutions occur—just like everyone else—because curiosity and persistence are not enough. If a curious and persistent person is upset or half asleep, solutions are not going to appear. What's most important at the time we are trying to solve a problem is the state of our consciousness. The wider awake we are, the brighter and calmer our consciousness is, the better we solve problems.

Behavior is another area often explored by scientists. Psychologists spend years investigating what kind of behavior talented people engage in, looking for the key to their *"aha"* experiences but, unfortunately, as we've seen in the case of Beethoven, Mozart, and others, it is impossible for any individual to undertake any specific type of behavior to solve a problem. Solutions always come unbidden and unforced. One day we drink five glasses of wine and have a solution and the next day the same five glasses produce nothing but a headache. One day, we walk through the woods and a solution appears and the next day we only get blisters. However, Graham Wallas, a British psychologist, in *The Art of Thought*[6] identified and described some general behavior associated with the task of problem solving. This behavior was divided by Wallas into four stages: 1.) Preparation, 2.) Incubation, 3.) Illumination, and 4.) Verification. Later, researchers identified and described an additional stage—we can number 2A.)—the propitious incident, which immediately precedes and initiates some solutions. Without doubt these five stages are related to the task of problem solving.

Mental preparation, which Wallas defines as that period when an individual is involved in studying a subject, is certainly necessary for solutions. Knowledge of math or astronomy is required for solving mathematical or astronomical problems.

Yet, as noted by Wallas, individuals intently working or studying most often are involved in other activities when a sought-after solution appears. These "other activities," the incubation stage, is described by Wallas as a more relaxed period. As in Beethoven or Mozart's case, when an individual is walking in the woods or riding in a carriage, that tranquil interlude provides the most conducive—*but far from certain*—conditions for an insight.

The more recently identified propitious incident stage denotes those accidental events that occasionally precede some illuminations. Newton seeing an apple fall before discovering gravity or Archimedes observing water rise in his bath before arriving at the principle of displacement are two famous examples of propitious incidents.

Although extremely brief, the "*aha*" moment itself is categorized by Wallas as a distinct stage. The illumination stage comprises the few seconds it takes for an insight to occur.

The verification stage is that mundane period after illumination when in some practical way, the individual confirms that the inspiration is correct. Not all "*ahas*" are right. Some are incomplete or just plain wrong.

> "...but above all is verification necessary. I have spoken of the feeling of absolute certitude accompanying the inspiration; in the cases cited this feeling was no deceiver, nor is it usually. But do not think this is a rule without exception; often this feeling deceives us without being any less vivid, and we only find it out when we seek to put on foot the demonstration."[7]
>
> **Henri Poincare—Mathematician**

However, while over the years these five stages have proved reliable in describing the outward pattern surrounding solutions, they do not, in any way, explain why these stages work or penetrate the inner mechanics of the illumination itself. They do not tell us with any accuracy or specificity how, why, or when a solution occurs. It is true anyone having an insight passes through these stages (although by definition only occasionally through the propitious incident stage), but it is also true that we can mimic the outward behavior described in these stages (which means the mental preparation and incubation stages) and yet not experience a single insight. We can study hard at any number of subjects, stroll on any manner of beaches, travel in any number of cars, carriages, or trains and still fail to find an answer because a solution is not caused by an outward pattern of behavior. A solution is caused by the inner behavior of consciousness.

Acknowledging the failure of personality and outward behavior to unveil the secret of solutions, many researchers turn to the physical structure of the brain. They confuse an understanding of the brain with an understanding of consciousness. Researchers look at how complex the brain is— millions of times more complicated than the most powerful computer—and think if they probe deeply enough into neurons, synapses, dendrons, axons, and all the other parts of the brain, eventually, they will discover the brain's role in solutions.

> Just like the letter "A" encoded in a computer circuit, your memory of your grandmother is not "contained" in one neuron—a "grandmother neuron," as opposed to, say, a "president of the United States" neuron. There is a vast network of (often distant) neurons that, in their connections with each other, collectively represent your grandmother memory.

> One particular neuron might perhaps encode a tiny memory fragment of your grandmother, let's say just one visual aspect of one particular facial contour. That is to say, that particular neuron will fire electrochemically when paired with visual input matching that contour. Nor is that one neuron dedicated solely to holding that piece of your grandmother memory; the same neuron probably participates in a great many other memories by virtue of its membership in a host of different connections with other arrays of neurons.[8]
>
> **Ralph Lewis—M.D.**

But no matter how complex the brain is—whether the brain has one cell, ten billion, or a billion billion—or how intricately the cells interact, the secret to solutions does not reside within the physical structure of the brain. Yes, the brain provides the hardware that allows our consciousness to function, but neurons on their own do not choose what we write about—whether it's the president of the United States or our grandmother.

Neurons are not the author of Hamlet. The "Jupiter" Symphony was not composed by amines and adrenaline. Synapses did not discover the laws of motion. Individual cells in the brain or groups of cells only receive, transmit, and record. A chemical or electric current does not question or reason. A chemical or electric current does not contemplate or examine. A chemical or electric current does not analyze or predict. A chemical or electric current does not evaluate or judge. A chemical or electric current has no interests, inventiveness, or inquisitiveness. The brain is a mechanical computing machine; consciousness is the force that animates and controls it. By themselves, the cells and the chemicals that make up the brain lack the desire, will, and sense of self to explore the mysteries of life and arrange the results into a specific order that becomes an idea or an insight.

The brain and consciousness function together as a unified whole, utilizing memory, senses, discrimination, desire, and will. However, it is that very intimacy between the mechanical functioning of the brain and consciousness that allows people to think that the brain is consciousness. But that idea is incorrect. Without consciousness, the brain is just inert flesh and blood. Consciousness enlivens it and gives it direction and purpose. Because the brain is physical, it is tempting to attribute all the qualities of consciousness to it, but equating the brain with consciousness is like equating a magnet with a magnetic field. It is true a magnetic field would not exist without the physical structure of the magnet but in substance and function they are different and obey different laws. Similarly, consciousness and the brain are inextricably linked, but in substance and function they are different and follow entirely different laws.

The physical machinery of the brain might be necessary to generate consciousness or, perhaps, as some people think, some form of universal consciousness is ultimately responsible for the physical machinery of the brain, but whichever is the case, the brain is not consciousness. Consciousness is not chemicals, cell tissue, or electrical impulses, however intricately arranged. The deeper scientists investigate the brain, the subtler the levels of the physiology they reach. Their efforts are something like Zeno's paradox where someone journeys from point A to point B but can only traverse half the distance at a time. Since every attempt is half way, the destination is never attained. Similarly, scientists always pierce deeper and deeper into the physical structure of the brain but their investigations never reach the abstract field of consciousness because another subtler layer of the physiology is always discovered in between.

Consciousness is a field of awareness in and of itself, and it is our consciousness that allows sensory input to register within our brain and acts as a unifying field, taking that input and organizing and connecting it. In order to think there has to be an "I," a unique awareness that knows of its own existence and can distinguish between it and other existences and wonder about the differences.

> So far, I have not mentioned a property that is certainly obvious to all humans who are conscious. We are conscious of being conscious.[9]
>
> **Gerald M. Edelman**
> **—Biologist and Author**

Attempting, perhaps, to get closer to our consciousness, some scientists seek the secret of solutions through the study of the thought process. They investigate whether the thoughts involved in creating solutions are simple or complex; verbal or visual; logical or intuitive. They examine thoughts from every angle but with little success because it is not individual thoughts, or any aspect of their relationship that causes thoughts to combine. What causes thoughts to connect is the field within which all thoughts occur and that field is consciousness.

Imagine an inventor or a mathematician researching a problem. At some point, he or she has all the correct information somewhere in his or her head. Yet the solution does not occur. Why? Because it is not individual thoughts that create the connection. *If our consciousness is weak, foggy, and disorderly, even though we have all the necessary information in our head, our thoughts remain muddled. If our consciousness is strong, clear, calm, and coherent, only then will thoughts combine into the correct answer.*

Consider Wallas' stages of illumination. What is the difference between the preparation and the incubation stage? By the end of the preparation stage all of the information necessary for a solution is gathered but the illumination does not take place. Why? Because a distinction exists between the state of our consciousness in the preparation stage and the state of our consciousness in the incubation stage. During the preparation stage our consciousness is busily engaged in the search for data. However, when we take a break (i.e., enter the incubation stage), and the state of our consciousness becomes calmer, fresher, and clearer, that is when the answer appears. Why? Because when our consciousness is bright, strong, and calm, it is better able to make the connections which are the solution. *Individual thoughts do not connect themselves. Individual thoughts combine into a solution only when there is an overall awareness capable of evaluating and arranging them, and that awareness, that organizing power is* **our consciousness.**

Picture our thoughts as iron filings scattered on a piece of paper. If we want to assemble the iron filings into an orderly pattern, what is the easiest method? It isn't fiddling with each iron filing or group of iron filings. To most easily arrange the iron filings simply place a magnet underneath the paper. Then, instantly, the iron filings align themselves into a systematic pattern produced by the magnet's magnetic field.

In the same way, what generates the connection of thoughts is not some quality within our thoughts or some aspect of their relationship, although these factors are important. Data that makes no sense when connected is not going to be combined. But it is not individual thoughts that create the connections. What drives our thoughts to connect is the field within which all thoughts occur: the field of consciousness. It is not that the meaning and relationship of thoughts are irrelevant. It is that the meaning and relationship of thoughts do not by themselves initiate or manage connections. That is the role of consciousness.

Our consciousness is the arranger. Our consciousness is the organizer. Our consciousness is the connector. When our consciousness is bright, orderly, and strong, it naturally merges our thoughts into the correct answer.

Intuitively, we all recognize that a strong, clear consciousness plays the primary role in creating solutions. For example, let's say one night we stay out too late and, in the morning, we crawl into our office with our eyes barely open and our brain aching with fatigue. What happens? We sit like a brick at our desk with our work piling ceiling-ward, not because our day's tasks are more difficult but because our consciousness is weaker. It is dull from lack of sleep and, as a result, we can't think well and we make lots of mistakes. In such a situation, we might wish we could slump down on our desk and doze, but we can't. We're at the office. We have research to do, clients to call, reports to write, decisions to make. However, the desire tugs at us. Why? Because after we've slept, we know our consciousness will be clearer and sharper and thus better able to solve problems.

Yet, when we're at our desk, missing the liveliness and brightness that an alert consciousness brings, even though we can't sleep, we still do something to improve the state of our consciousness. We stagger over to the expresso machine and drink our socially acceptable, all-too familiar, all-too addictive, all-too nerve jangling, caffeine-laden cup of coffee.

We drink our first cup. Our second. And our third. And to some extent the drug works. To quote a sign once posted in a Cambridge, Massachusetts ice-cream and coffee shop:

> …We want you to know that drinking any
> kind of coffee will improve your academic
> and athletic performance and improve

your chances of becoming something really special. MIT is hard. It's a lot harder if you're asleep.[10]

Coffee does make our consciousness more alert. (Even though our consciousness is not a chemical, chemicals do influence our brain and our brain projects that influence into our consciousness. Just like a magnetic field is not a magnet, but modifying the magnet's structure alters the magnetic field's strength, shape, and size):

> Caffeine's primary effects are...a temporary sense of well-being, a feeling of being "high," relief from fatigue, and stimulation of the nerves...[11]
> **Francis Sheridan Goulart—Author**

However, the beneficial changes from the caffeine are only temporary, and at some point, we slide back.

> [Stimulation} is followed by so-called secondary effects...from simple letdown to mental and physical depression...[12]
> **Francis Sheridan Goulart—Author**

Yet our reason for drinking coffee is positive. It's to help us solve problems because intuitively we all recognize that solutions occur within the field of our consciousness, and the livelier our consciousness is, the more effectively it organizes our thoughts into the correct answer. Thus, we try to adjust and/or artificially stimulate our consciousness to create the strongest, brightest, most alert state we can.

From caffeine, to amphetamines, to tranquilizers, to depressants, to antidepressants, to all the other chemicals legal and illegal which we ingest, we've all learned that if we're not happy with the current state of our consciousness, we can keep consuming chemicals until we get the condition—the clarity or lack of clarity—we want. Yet, obviously, none of these chemicals are good, and all of their effects are temporary except for the possible damage they do to our body.

But, nonetheless, the ubiquitous use of drugs does demonstrate that we're all willing and eager to change our consciousness wherever, whenever, and whatever way we can, if it will help us function better. However, rather than changing our awareness through drugs temporarily, superficially, and harmfully, we need to learn how to improve our consciousness naturally, permanently, and profoundly, and then utilize that improvement to help us solve problems.

CHAPTER 3

What is Consciousness?

Consciousness is a word that's used a lot these days but rarely very precisely. Most people, when they think of consciousness (if they think of consciousness at all) think of it as a vague and nebulous term, a buzzword of modern times. "Consciousness changing," "consciousness raising," and "consciousness expanding," are all trite phrases tossed about in speeches, books, and magazines. The truth is that most people who use these terms are not talking about consciousness. Rather, they are talking about various causes, concepts, concerns, philosophies, and pop-psychologies— subjects that fall more accurately under the category of "information," than consciousness. They are talking about the *news* that forests are in danger, rivers and oceans are polluted, and that the air is often bad to breathe; they are talking about the *hope* we abolish war, eliminate disease, and eradicate poverty; they are talking about the *belief* we're all created equal, we can all be what we want, and under the skin we're all one. They are talking about any number of ideas, causes, attitudes, moralities, and slogans for political, environmental, sociological, and psychological change, but they are not talking about consciousness.

Here, when we talk about consciousness, we mean something simpler and yet much more profound. Here when we talk about consciousness, we mean the awareness, the alertness, the brightness, the radiance, the luminosity that snaps on in the morning and signifies we are awake, we are alive, and that our brain is once more functioning and ready to experience. Here, when we talk about consciousness, we mean the liveliness, the force, the energy that is ourself, that we feel in our mind when sleep is gone and we're "up," thinking, speaking, and acting. Here when we talk about consciousness, we mean the existence, the being, the isness, the I-ness which is who and what we are—the experiencer, the perceiver, the observer who is identical to and indivisible from our awareness and gives us our sense of self.

Consciousness is not a logical argument, theory, concept, or philosophy. Consciousness is a reality. A quality. A substance. A thing. Just as light is invisible and untouchable, abstract yet real, consciousness is invisible and untouchable, abstract yet real. Just as light is a force and has a quality of its own—a force and quality that allows us to see even though we never see light. In the same way, consciousness is a force of its own and has a quality of its own—a force and quality that allows us to see, hear, taste, smell, and touch even though we never see, hear, taste, smell, or touch consciousness.

Consciousness allows us to learn; consciousness is not what is learned. Consciousness allows us to feel; consciousness is not our feelings. Consciousness allows us to act; consciousness is not our actions. Our thoughts, feelings, and actions change all the time. Yet no matter how much and how often they change, something inside us never changes. Something inside us is the same "*I*", the same self, the same experiencer, the same perceiver, the same observer, no matter what we feel, think, learn, or do. No matter how old or young we are. No matter when it is or where we are. And that something is our consciousness.

Consciousness and our thoughts are not inseparable. Consciousness and our thoughts are not woven together like a tapestry that can never be taken apart. Consciousness and our thoughts are more like a movie on a screen. To the eye, the movie and the screen are one. Yet the movie and the screen are different. The pure, white screen is necessary for images to appear. But the screen is separate from the images. When the movie is running, all we see are the images, not the screen. But if, for a moment, the movie stopped, the pure, white screen would become visible. Even when the movie is running the screen is present. The screen is always present.

Consciousness is like that screen. Our thoughts, feelings, and actions are like the movie. Consciousness is necessary for our thoughts, feelings, and actions to appear. But as soon as our thought, feelings, and actions appear, consciousness as if disappears. However, our consciousness is still present. Our consciousness is always present, and if for a moment our thoughts, feelings, and actions stopped, our consciousness would once more appear as what it is: silence, wakefulness, awareness, existence, being.

Another analogy:

Consciousness is like the ocean and our thoughts are like waves on the surface of the ocean. The waves are individualized aspects of the ocean like our thoughts are individualized aspects of our consciousness. When the waves roll across the surface of the ocean, they obscure the ocean. When our thoughts roll across the surface of our consciousness, our thoughts obscure our consciousness. But if for a moment the waves stopped, the flat, unbounded ocean would appear. In the same way, if, for a moment, our thoughts stopped, we would suddenly find ourself in a silent field of pure awareness, pure wakefulness, pure alertness, pure brightness, pure being—because that is who we are and what consciousness is.

We do not exist because we think. We think because we exist.

A thought is an object. A particle. A bit of data. A wisp of cerebration. One of many bits that float and twist and shift, constantly appearing and disappearing in our consciousness. Consciousness, awareness exists in and of itself as its own lively, pure field of being.

This distinction between our thoughts and our consciousness is very important and very real. Yet, for most of us, this distinction is neither understood nor experienced. For most of us, our thoughts, feelings, and perceptions continue in an endless swirl we can't turn off. When we think of who we are, we think of ourself as the unceasing whirlwind. We live our entire life in the movie—never knowing just below the surface lies the calm, clear, silent screen. But how often do we wish we could turn off our thoughts—that we could leave the fuss and bother of unwanted mental chatter, that we could for a moment just exist. Just be. Just experience a state of pure peacefulness. Pure calmness. Pure silence. It should be possible because our thoughts and our consciousness are not the same. No matter how many thoughts, feelings, and perceptions we have, just below the surface glistens the pure, serene, silent vastness of consciousness. Indeed, even though we may not realize it, we refer to our consciousness as a separate, distinct field all the time.

For instance, in the morning after a good night's sleep, when we say, "Today my mind feels bright and clear," to what are we referring? What is bright and clear? Is it any one thought or group of thoughts? No. Because that morning *all* our thoughts are bright and clear. Rather, the brightness and clarity is the property of the field within which all our thoughts occur: our consciousness. Or on other days, when we have a poor night's sleep and we say, "This morning my mind feels dull and foggy," again to what do we refer? Is the dullness and fogginess the property of any one thought or group of thoughts? No. Because that morning *all* our thoughts are dull and foggy. Rather, the dullness and fogginess belong to the field within which every thought occurs: our consciousness. On a bright and clear day all objects appear bright and distinct and on a dull and foggy day, the same objects appear dull and hazy. The brightness or dullness is not a quality of the objects. The brightness or dullness is a quality of the light. Similarly, the brightness or dullness within our mind is never due to our thoughts. It is always due to the field which contains our thoughts—the field of our consciousness. As in a lit room, we never spend our time analyzing the light, we only pay attention to the objects lit by the light, so within our mind, we never spend our time analyzing our consciousness, we only pay attention to the thoughts, feelings, and perceptions "lit" by our consciousness. However, it is our consciousness that is truly critical. It is our consciousness that generates the clarity or lack of clarity of our thoughts.

Consciousness is that self-illuminant, lively field of pure wakefulness, that glistening, knowing field of pure *I-ness*, that lively, luminescent field of pure *me-ness*, that inexhaustible, radiant field of pure transcendental being that animates and makes possible all our mental, emotional, and sensual life. Yet because of its abstractness, because it is obscured by thoughts, feelings, and perceptions, consciousness, which is the basis of our existence, in fact is our existence, is actually the most doubted, the most neglected, and the least understood aspect of our existence. It is this failure to recognize our consciousness as an independent, distinct field which causes us to neglect the most fundamental level of our thinking, the most fundamental level of our self, the most fundamental level of our being, and the most fundamental level of solutions.

CHAPTER 4

Do Robots, Androids, and Cyborgs Have Consciousness?

(NOTE: A robot is a machine that performs human-like tasks. An android is a robot designed with human features. A cyborg is a human being who has robot parts. However, science fictions books and films rarely concern themselves with proper definitions. Thus, the Terminator is a very advanced android, not a cyborg. Robocop is a true cyborg. But for this chapter these distinctions do not matter—except a cyborg with a human brain will have consciousness and a robot and an android will not.)

Many intelligent people, particularly in hi-tech, believe someday scientists and engineers will put together lots of very fast processors, wires, millions and millions of lines of code, throw in a dash of inspiration, enclose it in some sort of silicone, metal, and plastic frame, and end up with a conscious entity. This expectation is false.

We may create a robot or android that can talk, walk, add, subtract, and do many, many things faster and better than a human being. The robot or android may look like a human being, act like a human being, and in many ways think like a human being but, that does not mean the robot or android is conscious.

Thoughts are *not* consciousness. This confusion between thoughts and consciousness is perhaps why people believe a robot can gain consciousness. If one believes "thinking" is consciousness, then who is to say that a robot that can perfectly mimic thinking is not conscious? But consciousness is being. Pure existence. Pure awareness. Thinking is a mechanical activity. A very subtle form of activity but mechanical activity nonetheless. Words are objects. They have structure. They have form. They have meaning. When they are arranged to convey an idea, they follow patterns and rules. We can create software that copies these patterns and rules, but consciousness itself is beyond thought—it is being. Thus, ascribing consciousness to a robot because it can calculate, read, speak, distinguish, and choose is a mistake. For a robot to gain consciousness, it has to be capable of experiencing its own awareness and know it is experiencing its own awareness. While human beings can create robots that mimic thinking, they cannot make robots that experience their own awareness, their own being because they do not have "being." A robot is a machine created by human beings that is very good at imitating human beings. A robot or android will never have its own "I", its own "me", its own self that resides within its own consciousness. Wires, processors, and computer code can create a "thinking" machine but they cannot create consciousness.

In 1950, Alan Turing, the famous British computer scientist, invented what is called the Turing Test, which measures machine intelligence. The idea behind the test is to see if a machine in a different room can fool a human questioner into believing the machine is a human being. Science fiction books and movies sometimes use the Turing Test as a device to show that a computer has consciousness. But in reality, even if it passes the test, a machine is not conscious. It might say it is conscious but those are just words. Is the robot or android conscious of being conscious? Underneath its thinking apparatus is there a field of pure awareness? Or is it just very good at mimicking speech? It may be programmed to comprehend language and respond to questions but the machine is only a very clever construction run by electricity that can be disconnected or shut off. When it is unplugged, it is "off." When it is reconnected to its power source, it is "on." But it will never lose or regain consciousness because it never had consciousness.

Anthropomorphism is defined by Wikipedia as "the attribution of human traits, emotions or intentions to non-human entities. It is considered to be an innate tendency of human psychology," which is true. Children imbue their stuffed animals, dolls, and toy soldiers with human life. We talk to them, play with them, and, in some cases, believe they talk back. This behavior changes little when we grow older. We just talk to different objects. Adults talk to their cars, their TVs, their toasters, and their computers—and we do not mean voice commands; we mean actual conversation with inanimate objects. The more often a person interacts with an object, the more "lifelike" the object becomes and the more human attributes we assign to that object. So, it is no surprise that people would imbue a machine that's designed to look, act, and think like a human being with consciousness.

But no matter how sophisticated computers grow—and over time computers and robots will grow very, very sophisticated—they're still machines programmed by human beings to function like human beings. Whether a robot can "learn" or "think" doesn't matter. These skills are created by human intelligence. Even if the robot can recognize patterns and images, "solve" problems, and create art, it does these acts in accordance with its programming, and executing a very cleverly designed software program is not a sign of consciousness.

We love R2-D2 and C3PO but they are characters in *Star Wars* and like the dozens and dozens of other movie robot, android, and cyborg characters, are make-believe. Arnold Schwarzenegger is a human being. The Terminator is a character in a movie. Some dolls have a limited vocabulary and can "talk" but they are not conscious. *Toy Story* is a movie. Dolls and stuffed animals do not come to life when we leave the room. Nor do robots.

CHAPTER 5

Where Does Consciousness Come From?

Even though consciousness is undoubtedly real, powerful, and vital to everyone's existence, in fact, is everyone's existence, we who are it, live it, experience it every day all day long, have nothing but guesses as to its origin.

Many religions speak with certainty about the origin of consciousness, but if one is not religious or belongs to a different religion or a less dogmatic religion, the origin of consciousness remains unclear. Philosophers are full of arguments and speculations but they are just that: arguments and speculations. Scientists fare little better. However, since in this chapter we are analyzing the origin of consciousness, we can group all the various theories into four possibilities:

1. Consciousness is the creation of a divine being.
2. Consciousness is the result of evolution and came into existence when the brain came into existence.
3. Consciousness is an eternal, universal life force, and human beings, the brain, and indeed all matter emerged from it.
4. Consciousness is an eternal, universal life force and, along with it, some fundamental form of matter has always existed. The universe and everything in it, including human beings are the

result of the interplay between consciousness and this fundamental form of matter.

Possibility 1 is perhaps the easiest to discuss because consciousness as the result of a divine being is the end of the story or perhaps more accurately the beginning of the story. Those who want to believe in consciousness as the result of a divine being will and those who don't won't. Arguments for and against exist but in the face of belief, arguments are irrelevant. For us, the most important fact is that the origin of consciousness from a divine being does not interfere with our analysis of consciousness and the "*aha*" experience. If, as in religious stories, the universe begins with a divine being who creates men and women and infuses them with life that reality does not invalidate how our consciousness functions. God, as the Creator, still leaves us with our current reality. Nothing about our consciousness changes. Nothing about the "*aha*" experience changes. All the principles that we enumerate in this book remain the same. In terms of the truth of religious creation stories, it is enough that many people believe them and they are one possible theory.

However, one point about creation stories deserves mention. Whenever skeptics challenge creation stories, they tend to set up strawmen of the most literal biblical interpretations and then challenge those strict interpretations and think that in some way they have gained a victory. Yes, some religious followers believe in very literal interpretations, giving these doubters what they feel is the license to make their argument. For example, The Lord creating the universe in seven days, particularly in the light of modern science, is hard to believe. But while it should be incredibly obvious— nonetheless it is often overlooked—if a divine being created the universe, He began *before* the universe was created. Therefore, time as we know it did not exist. In a "time" before "time" what does "seven days" mean? We live in our own solar system and have our day and year regulated by the Earth, rotating around the Sun. But why would an infinite, omnipotent being use an Earth-day to regulate His work, particularly before the Earth even exists? And when the Earth and our solar system finally do come into existence, they are specks in a tiny corner of our tiny galaxy tucked away in a tiny corner of the universe, and it is ridiculous to think of an eternal, omnipresent, omnipotent Being as bound by a twenty-four-hour Earth-day. When God begins to create the Universe and time comes into existence, God's-day could last billions of years. Thus, mocking the biblical creation story because it states that God produced the universe in seven "days" is not logical, accurate, or fair. A day before a twenty-four-hour Earth-day existed is not a day as we know it. Also, the Hebrew word for day (*yom*), like the English word "day," can be used to stand for more than a twenty-four-hour day. *Yom* can mean an epoch like "The Day of the Dinosaur" or it can mean a period of light as opposed to a period of darkness.[13] All of which doesn't mean that the creation story is true or untrue. It just means that the creation story has more potential as a description of creation than is granted by skeptics, as well as those religious thinkers who are literal in their interpretations.

Possibility 2 follows current scientific thinking—matter originates from a cosmic Big Bang billions of years ago. After this cosmic explosion, galaxies, solar systems, and our planet slowly form and billions of years later, seas appear on Earth, and in another billion or so years, one-celled creatures swim around, and more billions of years later, fishlike creatures wade out of the ocean, stretch, dry off, and continue their evolutionary adventure on land. In this scenario, since consciousness is a manifestation of the brain, consciousness comes into existence when the brain comes into existence.

Possibility 2 means that, as far as we know, consciousness is an isolated and rare phenomenon restricted to brain—based beings on Earth.

Scientists say they have traced the origin of the Big Bang back to milliseconds after the theoretical explosion. Unfortunately, in the field of physics, a gap of a few milliseconds is big enough to fit in all of eternity. Veiled in even greater mystery is the scientific explanation of how life appeared on Earth. The further back we go, the less hard evidence there is. Researchers on the origin of life are like the scientists in *Jurassic Park*. Whenever there is some missing dinosaur DNA, Jurassic Park geneticists throw in a strand of frog DNA. Today's scientists, whenever there is a gap in their knowledge, toss in a few billion years and, like Dr. Frankenstein (to use another work of fiction), a couple of lightning bolts, and, poof, a one-celled beastie emerges—alive!

> The classic 1952 Miller–Urey experiment and similar research demonstrated that most amino acids, the chemical constituents of the proteins used in all living organisms, can be synthesized from inorganic compounds under conditions intended to replicate those of the early Earth. Scientists have proposed various external sources of energy that may have triggered these reactions, including lightning and radiation.[14]

For inanimate matter to transform into animate beings takes an amazing string of coincidences, even for a universe billions of years old. The reality is science does NOT know how the universe originated or how life on earth arose or how consciousness came into existence, so scenario 2, although widely believed, is only one of the four possibilities.

Possibility 3 involves a universal consciousness (not necessarily a god or God, just an awareness, a force, being), which has always existed and will always exist. Even though we are trained to ask why, there does not have to be a why. This universal consciousness always was, always is, and always will be.

At first glance, of course, an eternal, universal consciousness seems impossible, but frankly all four scenarios seem impossible. Yet here we are—billions of us, milling around on the planet, the sole sentient creatures in a trillion, trillion, trillion miles of space, so one of the four scenarios has to be true.

In Possibility 3 an abstract, infinite field of consciousness somehow spawns the material universe and at least one planet teeming with life. In this possibility's favor an infinite, eternal, abstract field of consciousness has two things going for it: 1.) As abstract as it is, consciousness is something, so when matter begins, it isn't appearing out of nothing, and 2.) Consciousness is, at least, conscious. It is being. It is lively. So, if consciousness can somehow create matter, it is not as huge a leap for that matter to eventually evolve to reflect consciousness.

But the question remains, how does an abstract field of consciousness, infinite and eternal though it may be, create matter?

Awareness is the key.

Since consciousness exists as a lively field of awareness and that field of awareness is all that there is, we must ask— what is this field of awareness aware of? Awareness has to become aware of something. As there is nothing else, the only answer is: this infinite field of awareness becomes aware of itself. And awareness knowing itself is The Beginning. When this infinite field of awareness becomes aware of itself, suddenly something happens. Awareness as if breaks. Where once we had one element, awareness, we now have three.

Our first element is awareness: the observer—awareness observing itself. Our second element is awareness: the object—

awareness is what is being observed. Our third element is awareness: the action—awareness engaged in observing itself. Thus, from one infinite field of pure, silent being suddenly we have three elements, interacting within itself: awareness, the observer; awareness, the observed; awareness, the action of observation. From these three elements, all the qualities of relative existence unfold.

Unbounded awareness becoming aware of itself must take place over time. Even if it is a very small fraction of time, it is still time. It is a sequence of events.

The act of observation creates space. An observation has to take place over a certain distance, otherwise it isn't an observation. It doesn't matter how small a distance. It is a distance.

Observation is an action. It is a very subtle form of action, but it is an action. Being is no longer motionless as it was in its abstract, pure state. It is doing something. It is observing.

With action energy comes into existence. Action requires energy like propelling the wheels of a car, and action creates energy like the wheel of a dynamo producing electricity. In either case, if action occurs, energy exists.

Observation also creates an object—a point. Something that's observable. Whether it's infinitely small or infinitely large, it is a thing.

Therefore, from one abstract field of pure consciousness, we now have Time, Space, Energy, Motion, and some quasi form of matter—that point.

In addition, when we talk of the "breaking" of unbounded, abstract consciousness, it is such a vast, infinite field. When consciousness breaks into Time, Space, Energy, Motion, and Matter, that break does not necessarily happen once. Infinite awareness is infinite and can become aware of itself an infinite number of times, potentially creating an infinite amount of points, an infinite amount of space, an infinite amount of motion, an infinite amount of energy, *and* an infinite amount of heat. Heat is another quality made from the breaking of this Universal Consciousness.

> All matter is made of tiny particles called atoms, molecules and ions. These tiny particles are always in motion—either bumping into each other or vibrating back and forth. It is the motion of particles that creates a form of energy called heat (or thermal) energy that is present in all matter.[15]

Thus, from our one still, silent field of pure awareness, we have a cauldron of vibrating, seething, bubbling, breaking infinity that bears a poetic similarity to what physics talks about when it describes the universe emerging from a field of pure potentiality.

> String theory posits that at the beginning of the universe (up to 10^{-43} seconds after the Big Bang), the four fundamental forces were once a single fundamental force. According to string theory, every particle in the universe, at its most microscopic level (Planck Length), consists of varying combinations of vibrating strings (or strands) with preferred patterns of vibration. String theory further claims that it is through these specific oscillatory patterns of strings that a particle of unique mass and force charge is created (that is to say, the electron is a type of string that vibrates one way, while the up quark is a type of string vibrating another way, and so forth).[16]

Of course, poetic similarities do not mean truth, but we have, at least, a vision of how matter could form from an abstract field of consciousness. And when over eternity (or in just one instant), consciousness becomes aware of itself millions, billions, and trillions of times, the resulting boiling of time, space, motion, energy, and heat could give birth to something like the Big Bang, spawning galaxies, solar systems, and our planet. On our planet, oceans and continents could gradually form, and cells, plants, and other living creatures could one day inundate the seas and land. In this scenario, consciousness already pervades the universe, so when beings develop brains and tread the earth, it is a lot less remarkable when they gain consciousness and seek again to know themselves and their origin.

Possibility 4 is interesting because it resolves many of the leaps we have to make in Possibilities 1, 2, and 3. In Possibility 4, matter and consciousness always exist and will always exist. Consciousness does not have to create matter and matter does not have to create consciousness. The existence of consciousness is an eternal miracle. The existence of matter is an eternal miracle. Like Possibility 3, there is no question. There is no answer. There is no why. It is because it is.

As in Possibility 3, infinite awareness has to become aware of itself. Awareness always becomes aware of itself. That's what awareness does. But in this scenario, there is also something else. Instead of just becoming aware of itself, awareness becomes aware of whatever subtle form of matter exists. This matter that eternally exists is NOT planets, stars, and solar systems. We know they evolve. The matter that eternally exists can very well be whatever subtle form of matter scientists believe lurked in the Primordial Vastness before the Big Bang. Then, perhaps, in some interaction between this lively field of infinite awareness awakening to itself *and* awakening to this very subtle infinite (or almost infinite) form of matter, the Big Bang is triggered and the universe unfolds just as scientists propose. However, since consciousness already exists, once more it is a lot less remarkable when, eventually, the human brain gains the ability to reflect consciousness.

But whether or not this fourth possibility (or the first, second, or third) is true, we do know the end result. *We* are the end result. Human beings and human consciousness eventually exist. Whatever our beginning (take your choice), our consciousness is our consciousness is our consciousness. How the universe forms is speculation. Our consciousness is not speculation. We are here. We are aware. We are the miracle and the miracle is real. For the rest of this book whenever we talk about consciousness, we will not mean any kind of speculative universal consciousness, we will mean our own individual consciousness, which is the basis of our life and is the basis of solutions.

CHAPTER 6

Principles of How Our Consciousness Functions

If consciousness is real (which it undoubtably is), no matter how subtle and abstract a field it is, it must behave according to consistent and orderly principles that we can discover and know. It's not as if our heart, lungs, blood, skin, kidneys, and stomach perform in a systematic and coherent manner and that at the gates of the mind we leave the world of order, regulation, and truth and enter the world of chaos. Consciousness is not anything we pretend it to be or make up what we think it should be or decide by consensus. Just as every nerve, cell, muscle, and bone behaves according to precise, orderly principles, so does our consciousness.

In fact, our consciousness behaves in a more precise, more systematic, and more orderly way than any other part of our body or, for that matter, any other part of nature. It has to because our consciousness is responsible for our ability to make sense out of everything in nature. It is absurd to believe that our consciousness—the field which is responsible for our ability to think, feel, and act, which is responsible for our ability to observe, calculate, weigh, measure, understand, and create—is in itself a field of disorder and confusion. Indeed, if consciousness did not function according to exact and definite principles, how could we know anything? If the basis of our ability to experience were random then our thoughts, feelings, and actions would be random and we could not function, never mind function in a coherent manner. But we do function, and we do know, and we do create, and more than that, we have a continuity and a universality in our functioning.

From second to second, from hour to hour, from year to year, we maintain and build on what we've learned. We don't forget who we are or what we've accomplished. Our consciousness does not behave differently from person to person or from place to place. Consciousness does not act one way in Oklahoma and another in Texas; one way in Florida and another in Washington. Consciousness does not behave differently for males or females, Europeans or Asians. Just as every heart, lung, bone, and cell works according to specific laws, consciousness obeys specific laws.

Every consciousness is capable of thinking and experiencing and does so in a similar fashion. Every consciousness uses a language for similar purposes and with similar results. When we awaken and are aware, our consciousness is the same whether we are Italian, English, Chinese, or French. The subject matter of our thoughts might differ. The objects we see might differ. Our feelings might differ. Our words might differ, but our awareness does not alter because at its basis consciousness is a field of pure awareness and in its pure state it has no variation or individuality.

As in the analogy of the movie screen, images change from movie to movie, but the screen is always the same. Or in the analogy of the ocean, the waves change from minute to minute, but the ocean is the same. So, with our awareness, thoughts, feelings, and perceptions change from day to day, but the underlying field of consciousness is always the same. And if consciousness is always the same, if consciousness is governed by principles that are precise, orderly, systematic, and universal, then from analyzing our own consciousness we can determine what these principles are and how we can apply these principles to discover the secret to solutions.

Principles of Consciousness

One: consciousness is. It exists. It is a field of pure awareness.

Two: consciousness as a field of pure awareness is separate from our thoughts, feelings, and perceptions. As we discussed, being and thinking are two separate qualities. We have to be awake in order to think. Consciousness can exist without thoughts but thoughts cannot exist without consciousness.

Three: consciousness is not only separate from, but is the source of all our mental activity. As thoughts cannot exist without our consciousness, every thought, feeling, hearing, taste, touch, and perception begins within the field of our consciousness. Perhaps we are in the habit of considering input from our senses as originating externally but until a sensory experience registers within the field of our consciousness, for us that sensory experience does not exist.

Four: consciousness functions according to principles that are universal, permanent, and knowable. As consciousness functions everywhere the same, it is universal. Because consciousness functions consistently over time—within our own life and the life of those before and after us—it is permanent. As consciousness is a state of awareness, it is obviously knowable. A field of awareness that provides the basis of knowing everything is capable of knowing itself.

Five: our consciousness is orderly. In fact, our consciousness is a field of pure order. It *has* to be a field of pure order.

If consciousness exists as a field of pure awareness independent of and separate from our thoughts, feelings, and perceptions, it has nothing within it other than itself. Void of all objects, consciousness has no duality. Like the one white glistening screen all it consists of is itself which in its pure wholeness, in its pure brightness, in its pure undifferentiated oneness is completely homogenous and orderly.

In Chapter Five, we discussed the possibility of a universal consciousness "breaking." But while the concept of a universal consciousness is speculation, our individual consciousness is not. Which leads us to a profound paradox. On the one hand, consciousness is an undifferentiated field of wholeness; on the other hand, consciousness is a field of awareness and, as a field of awareness, our own individual consciousness must also "break." Wakefulness is our basic state: we are aware, we are awake. However, the nature of awareness is to become aware of something and that first something our consciousness becomes aware of is always our self: awareness becoming aware of its own awareness.

As quoted earlier:

> So far, I have not mentioned a property that is certainly obvious to all humans who are conscious. We are conscious of being conscious.[17]

From "being" (existing) to "I am being" (being aware of our own existence) is in essence every individual's first thought. But it happens so spontaneously and innocently, we are barely aware of having the thought.

Our consciousness is aware and we know that we are aware. We know and we know that we know.

However, even when our individual consciousness "breaks," our consciousness is still orderly because the process by which consciousness breaks is orderly. 1.) our consciousness is a field of awareness—the observer; 2.) our consciousness is the object observed: our me, our I, our self; and 3.) our consciousness is engaging in the process of observation—the action of becoming aware of our own existence.

This orderly process of our awareness as the knower, what is known, and the process of knowing serves as the foundation for how our consciousness knows anything— except what is known changes from our own individual self to objects around us.

For thousands and thousands of years, human civilization has built on this foundation through language, art, philosophy, history, mathematics, and science. These disciplines are the precise, systematic, and orderly tools our consciousness has developed to measure, explore, and understand ourselves and everything around us. But all this "knowing" is based on this orderly tripart structure: our own awareness becoming the knower; the object our awareness becomes aware of; and our awareness engaging in the process of observation.

For example, if we are thinking, our consciousness is the thinker. Then, there is the object—what we are thinking. Finally, there is the action—the process of thinking. This tripart process all occurs within the field of our own consciousness, which leads to our sixth principle, which states that consciousness has energy. The observer, the object observed, and the act of observation describe activity. It is a very subtle form of activity but nonetheless it is activity, and since activity cannot exist without energy, we can say consciousness has energy.

In nature the subtlest levels of matter have more energy than grosser levels. Atomic energy is more powerful than chemical energy. Chemical energy is more powerful than kinetic energy. *Thought energy* is a very subtle form of energy but very real and powerful. Every painting, symphony, engine, rocket, computer, building, city, and nation begins as a thought. It is true, we have stated that our consciousness and our thoughts are separate, but although separate, thoughts are still activity taking place within our own consciousness. Since our thoughts have their source within the field of our consciousness, the energy contained in our thoughts originates from within our consciousness. And if consciousness contains energy, our seventh principle is that consciousness is creative.

Energy creates. Anything which has energy has at least the potential to be creative—to give rise to that which is new, which is what creativity is. Certainly, in the absence of energy, such as when we are tired or in deep sleep, nothing gets done. As we gain energy, we gain the ability to act and achieve. An alert and functioning consciousness always generates new plans, new ideas, new goals. Even the youngest children when awake endlessly move, act, and achieve. Consciousness, awareness, wakefulness is lively and that liveliness and energy *create*.

Usually when we use the word creativity, we mean composing a symphony or writing a play. When we use creativity in that sense what we're really talking about is energy *combined* with intelligence. When we write a poem, we need the energy to generate thoughts and we need the intelligence to direct, choose, and transform those thoughts into words and meanings.

Creativity and intelligence are separate qualities. Creativity is energy. Intelligence is the ability to discriminate— to analyze differences, to maintain a direction, to choose between object A and object B. But the distinction between creativity and intelligence is often blurred. Intelligence is most often presumed to be a part of creativity. This combining of the qualities of creativity and intelligence into the one word "creativity" is not "wrong." For example, in the title of this book *The Solution System: A Journey into Consciousness and Creativity*, we use the term "creativity," as how it is most generally understood: the merging of the qualities of energy and intelligence. But when analyzing the qualities of consciousness, we need to be as accurate as possible, and consider creativity and intelligence as intimate but yet separate partners. Therefore, our eighth principle states: consciousness is intelligent.

If something has the potential to move in any direction, yet uses its power of discrimination to maintain a specific direction to accomplish an overall purpose or goal, it is intelligent. Creativity is the raw energy that begins and sustains a process and intelligence is the decision maker, the evaluator, the discriminator giving shape and purpose to what is created. However, while creativity and intelligence are indeed separate qualities, neither one is very much good without the other which is why their distinction is so often blurred. Without intelligence (direction), creativity (energy) is merely random motion and without creativity (energy), intelligence (direction) is merely purpose without the ability to move. Both qualities require each other and both qualities are fundamental aspects of consciousness, and when working together, give rise to all human progress and achievement.

With the combination of creativity and intelligence, we can accomplish a task. If we want to cook a meal, our creativity and intelligence directs us to gather the ingredients, mix them in the right proportion, and heat them on the stove. If we want to write a magazine article, our creativity and intelligence starts us on the first page and leads us word after word, sentence after sentence, paragraph after paragraph until we reach the last page. If we want to travel to Chicago, our creativity and intelligence steers us from wherever we are to walk, bike, run, ride, or fly, not to Milwaukee, New York, or Phoenix, but to Chicago.

However, while creativity is the energy to move and intelligence is the power to maintain a specific direction, we need to add a very important ninth principle which is that our consciousness has "depth." When we talk of "depth" in relation to our consciousness, it means our consciousness not only has the ability to "move" on its surface level from idea to idea to idea but consciousness also has the ability to "move within."

We've already alluded to this phenomenon without specifically describing it. When we stated that consciousness is like a movie on a screen—our thoughts are the movie, the screen is pure consciousness—we are implying there is a distance between the movie and the screen. This distance indicates depth. We also discussed consciousness as an ocean with waves on the surface and the calm silent ocean below. As waves have height, this height also indicates distance—the space between the height of the waves and the body of the ocean. Finally, there is the distance (or depth) between the waveless surface of the ocean and the bottom of the ocean.

While these images are just analogies, we all experience that sometimes our thoughts move as if horizontally along the surface of our consciousness from thought to thought to thought, and sometimes we experience our consciousness as if diving deeper, exploring one particular idea in a much more profound and consuming way. The common word we use to describe this phenomenon is "absorption."

This experience of absorption is not rare or special. We experience absorption many times every day—when we're reading a book, when we're watching TV, when we're working, and when we're just "deep" in thought. During an experience of absorption, we lose awareness of our surroundings and we lose track of time. We all have experienced a book we couldn't put down, or a video game we couldn't stop playing, or a tv series we binge-watched. Even when we have other things to do or need to go to sleep, we don't because the book or the game or the TV show is so *absorbing*. Another aspect of this experience of absorption is that if we're suddenly interrupted, we feel as if we've "popped" back up to the surface, which also demonstrates this ninth principle: that our consciousness has depth.

But what motivates our consciousness to move within? We become absorbed in so many things every day. But why? This question leads us to our tenth principle which is that the direction our consciousness most naturally, innocently, and effortlessly moves in *is the direction of greater charm.*

One way to interpret this phrase, "the direction of greater charm," is if, for instance, we're at a library and there are two rooms ahead, one of which contains books on chemistry (which we hate), the other of which contains books on history (which we love), our consciousness will naturally direct us into the room containing the history books. Whenever our consciousness has a choice between something charming or something less charming, its tendency will be to choose the direction which has the greater charm. This example is a simple "surface level" demonstration of the principle of our consciousness moving in the direction of greater charm. However, an example of this principle on a subtler, more profound level is that once we start reading a history book, if it indeed is "charming," our consciousness very quickly becomes "absorbed" in the book. It captivates our entire attention and we "sink" into the book. We lose awareness of our surroundings and of time because our consciousness has this characteristic which we are labeling as "depth."

When we're bored or when the subject is dull, our consciousness remains on the surface. When we're interested or when we're charmed, our consciousness goes deep. We *never* become absorbed in something we don't like. Our consciousness only becomes absorbed in something that is charming, and the depth of our absorption is directly proportional to the charm of the object. The greater the charm, the greater the depth of the absorption. The process of absorption is so natural and effortless that when it happens, we're not even aware that it is happening. If, for example, we're reading a book and someone calls our name and we feel as if our awareness pops back up, this popping back up is when, for the first time, we realize the depth of our absorption which shows how natural, effortless, and spontaneous the experience is. We only realize the depth of our absorption *after* the experience is over, which inexorably leads us to our eleventh principle.

Our eleventh, and last principle in this chapter, states that when our consciousness moves in the direction of greater charm, it moves in the direction of greater charm *by itself*. This little phrase, "by itself," is very important. It establishes that the ability to move in the direction of greater charm is an inherent part of consciousness and does NOT come from our will. When our consciousness is absorbed do we tell our consciousness to become absorbed like a captain ordering a submarine to dive? No. Our absorption occurs spontaneously by the nature of consciousness itself. Yes, we sit down. Yes, we open the book and, yes, we start to read. These tasks are performed by our will. But the process of absorption occurs *by the nature of consciousness itself*. When we're reading an interesting book, we don't even realize how deeply immersed in the book we are until someone calls our name or shakes us out of our "spell" and we pop back up. This unawareness of our absorption shows that the phenomenon of consciousness moving in the direction of greater charm occurs not by any intention of our own but due to our consciousness' own nature.

To demonstrate this point even more clearly, let's look at it from the opposite angle. Instead of reading an interesting book, let's say, for whatever reason, we have to read fifty pages of a dull book.

When dutifully we start reading the dull book, as far as we're concerned, we're reading the book. This is what we told our consciousness to do and this is what our consciousness is doing. But, as we all experience, the moment our mental control slips (which with a boring book doesn't take very long), our consciousness shifts from the dull book to something more enjoyable like a daydream—maybe about what we're going to do on the weekend. Then, we remain absorbed in the daydream until, perhaps, our phone rings or someone walks in, and it is only at this point that we realize we're NOT reading the dull book but lost in the daydream. However, we only become aware of the shift from the first object (the book) to the second object (the daydream) AFTER it occurs. This shows that the movement of consciousness in the direction of greater charm occurs by itself *due to an independent intelligence inherent within our own consciousness.*

While we're used to our physical bodies functioning with autonomous flesh and blood computerlike regulators—our heart beats on its own, our lungs breathe on their own, our stomach digests on its own, our immune system fights disease on its own—we're not used to thinking of our consciousness functioning with its own autonomous built-in computerlike regulators, but it does. Because of our body's physical nature, it's easy to accept the existence of independent, mechanical intelligences because who wants to bother spending all day (or worse, all night), supervising the beating of our heart, the breathing of our lungs or the digesting of our food? It requires no great stretch of the imagination to acknowledge both the reality and the value of having independent, automatic, self-operating intelligences running the mechanical affairs of our body.

But for ourself—our I, our me, our experiencer who resides in consciousness, who is consciousness—it's more difficult to think of any aspect of our own consciousness as having a mechanical nature capable of functioning independently. Consciousness is so abstract and so intimate; so much of who and what we are. However, just as with our body, we can move our hands and limbs and yet we do not control the growth of our bones or our skin, so with our consciousness we can think what we want and place our attention where we want—we can think about geography or history or politics—but after setting our consciousness in a particular direction or on a particular task, only if our consciousness finds that task or direction charming will it continue in that task or direction. Once our consciousness becomes bored, due to its own nature, our consciousness shifts to something more enjoyable. Due to our consciousness' own inner intelligence, it spontaneously becomes absorbed in an object if it's interesting and spontaneously drifts away from an object if it's dull. What our eleventh principle simply makes clear is this independent, intelligent, autonomous behavior.

Thus, having delineated these eleven principles, we can see that even though consciousness is a simple field, it is a complex field capable of behaving in complex ways. Like light which is in itself colorless yet reflects many colors, our awareness is one, pure homogeneous whole, yet it is capable of exhibiting many diverse qualities and acting in many diverse ways.

CHAPTER 7

The Nature of Charm Is Doing Less and Accomplishing More

We've now established that our consciousness when left on its own moves in the direction of greater charm. But what we haven't discussed is on what basis our consciousness decides one direction is more charming than another.

Since charm, happiness, and enjoyment are subjective judgements, we might think that to answer this question requires long aesthetic arguments. However, that is not the case. While it is true as individuals we all have different likes and dislikes, when we consider our consciousness simply as a field of pure awareness, the basis for the movement of our consciousness in the direction of greater charm can be expressed very simply: what our consciousness finds charming is anything that uses a minimum of energy to accomplish the maximum that it can, or stated more colloquially, anything that does less and accomplishes more. Again, subject to the idiosyncrasies of our likes and dislikes. The most beautifully written poem can bore someone who hates poetry and a mathematical equation that expresses a deep principle of nature can leave someone who hates math apathetic.

Imagine the delight we derive from a well-designed car that fulfills all our transportation needs, rarely breaks, and gets a lot of miles to the gallon or a well-designed house that has all the rooms placed where they are most convenient, closets that are the most useful size, and a hi-tech kitchen where all the appliances are most easy to reach.

Think how much we enjoy a tool that allows us to accomplish a difficult task with less effort, or a software program that is simple to use and accomplishes a complex project quickly or a well-engineered cellphone that is light, fast, and long lasting.

> Simplicity, clarity, singleness: these are the attributes that give our lives power and vividness and joy.[18]
> **Richard Halloway—Author**

This principle of doing less and accomplishing more is not only an objective description of the subjective experience of charm, it is a general principle of how all of nature functions. Everything in nature moves, breathes, grows, melds, reproduces, and dissolves in such a way that it does less and accomplishes more. Energy from the sun fuels the growth of plants and the same energy evaporates the oceans to make the rain that waters the plants. A flower's petals attract a bee to spread the flower's pollen and the same bee, while spreading the flower's pollen, gathers the nectar to make the honey which both the bee and we eat. Our skin holds us together and allows us to feel. A nose breathes air and smells food. Even in death our bodies fertilize the earth and serve as nourishment for other living beings. Nothing in nature is wasted. Nothing in nature is lost. Every part and particle— from a planet to an electron—expends the least amount of energy to accomplish the most that it can.

> Waste does not exist in nature because ecosystems reuse everything that grows

in a never-ending cycle of efficiency and
purpose.[19]

**Frans van Houten
—CEO, Royal Phillips**

Of all the motions that may bring a system
of material particles from a certain actual
position to a given final position (the total
energy remaining constant), the actual motion
is that for which the action is a minimum.[20]

Max Planck—Physicist

To a physicist, it is an intoxicating notion
that the vast storehouse of information of
our physical universe, painfully accumulated
over several thousands of years of careful
investigation, can be summarized in one
theory.[21]

**Michio Kaku and Jennifer
Thompson—Science Writers**

Nature operates in the shortest way possible.[22]

**Aristotle
—Philosopher and Scientist**

Physics is experience, arranged in economical
order.[23]

Ernst Mach—Physicist

All things being equal, the simplest solution
tends to be the best one.[24]

**William of Ockham
—Friar and Philosopher**

As eager participants in Nature's grand economy, we
humans try to imitate her efficiency. The poems, machines,
businesses, paintings, buildings, and philosophies, etc.

we produce are all conceived, designed, constructed, and considered successful if, and only if, they do less and accomplish more.

> Despite a lapse of twenty years (*Notorious*) is still a remarkably modern picture, with very few scenes and an exceptionally pure story line. In the sense that it gets a maximum effect from a minimum of elements, it's really a model of scenario construction...[25]
> **Francois Truffaut—Film Director**

> I like to get the most effect out of the fewest notes. This is getting back to the Mozart idea—simplicity in composition.[26]
> **George Gershwin—Composer**

> Perfection is achieved, not when there is nothing more to add, but when there is nothing left to take away.[27]
> **Antoine de Saint-Exuperey**
> **—Author**

> Not a wasted word. This has been a main point to my literary thinking all my life.[28]
> **Hunter S. Thompson**
> **—Author and Journalist**

> One merit of poetry few persons will deny: it says more and in fewer words than prose.[29]
> **Voltaire—Philosopher**

> We ascribe beauty to that which is simple; which has no superfluous parts; which exactly answers its end.[30]
> **Ralph Waldo Emerson**
> **—Author and Philosopher**

How many words would one need to write in order to explain everything the line means? The essence of its success is exactly that it says so much in so little. Every word counts: remove any one and the meaning is lost. A whole area of meaning has been reduced to what must certainly be the fewest possible words.[31]

John Ciardi—Poet and Critic

The higher processes of art are all processes of simplification…That is very nearly the whole of the higher artistic process: finding what conventions of form and what detail one can do without and yet preserve the spirit of the whole[32].

Willa Cather—Author

We could go on listing numerous such expressions of doing less and accomplishing more, but to do less and accomplish more here, we can best demonstrate the all-pervasiveness of the principle by introducing the first law of thermodynamics known as the conservation of energy, which declares, "Energy can be neither created nor destroyed. When a loss occurs in one form of energy, an equal increase occurs in other forms of energy."[33] Thus, in its most cosmic sense, this law means that in terms of energy, *the universe accomplishes everything by doing absolutely nothing.* The amount of energy in the Universe always remains the same. It just changes forms. And if we go from the cosmic to the more earthly realm of engineering, we see the same law stated in more practical terms.

It is impossible to construct an engine, operating in a cycle (that is, continuously) which does nothing other than take heat from a source and performs an equivalent amount of work.[34]

Arthur Beiser
—Author and Physicist

On this practical scale, the law states that we cannot completely transform one form of energy into another form of energy, and this inability *always creates waste.* But it is through "waste" that the principle of doing less and accomplishing more reveals itself most clearly.

For example, if a gallon of gas contains the potential to propel a car one hundred miles, in reality, the engine of transformation, the car's motor may only propel the car thirty miles. Due to the imperfection in the mechanics of transformation, the motor wastes energy. But since energy can neither be created or destroyed, the wasted energy does not disappear. In a car's engine, it appears as heat exhaust. Thus, the conservation of energy still holds. But this "waste" allows for the principle of doing less and accomplishing more to show itself. Someone can produce a car that travels thirty miles to the gallon, while someone else can design a car that "does less and accomplishes more" by driving a car forty miles to the gallon. The key to the concept is the engine of transformation. It is correct that energy is neither created nor destroyed, so if a gallon of gas contains the potential to power a car one hundred miles, because the engine of transformation never functions at maximum efficiency, the forty mile per gallon car "wastes" sixty miles of energy in heat exhaust. The conservation of energy holds but because the engine of transformation—that which takes one form of energy and changes it into another—is incapable of perfection, engines of transformation exist that are better (or worse) at doing less and accomplishing more. Those that do less and accomplish more are praised and rewarded and cause pleasure; engines of transformation that do more (use energy inefficiently) and accomplish less cause displeasure, are discarded, and forgotten.

Gas engines replaced horses. Jet engines replaced propeller driven piston engines. Oil heaters replaced wood stoves. Light bulbs replaced candles. Computers replaced typewriters. Electric car engines may soon replace gas engines. Throughout the ages, doing less and accomplishing more is always a crucial ingredient in the advancement of civilization. Everything we do, act, judge, decide, desire, and produce is motivated by doing less and accomplishing more. No one wants to buy (or create) a device that doesn't accomplish its task efficiently.

Let's look at this same principle on an even subtler scale. Let's look at the engine of transformation we call our consciousness. Much like any engine of transformation, our consciousness performs a task: it thinks. Depending how efficiently it performs that task, it either does less and accomplishes more (what we want) or does more and accomplishes less (what we don't want).

When our consciousness is in a whirl and our thoughts are confused, our consciousness does more but we accomplish very little (what we don't want). When our consciousness is calm and alert, our thoughts function with increased efficiency and we do less and accomplish more (what we want)—and of all the mental activity we undertake, the *"aha"* moment, the moment of solution, is the mental activity that best expresses doing less and accomplishing more because in just one flash all the numerous elements necessary for a solution connect, *and this experience always brings us pleasure.*

Whenever our consciousness does less and accomplishes more by arranging a few notes, words, colors, or numbers into a specific order which makes the notes a song, the words a poem, the colors a painting, and the numbers a mathematical equation, *the accomplishment always brings us pleasure. The*

*very shout of "eureka" or the gasp of "aha" expresses the intense
mental pleasure such experiences bring.*

When these epiphanic moments are described by artists,
scientists, entrepreneurs, and philosophers the words which
they most often choose: "flash," "light," "fire," "blaze,"
"illumination," "joy," "delight," "charm," happiness,"
"bliss," serve to both substantiate the abstract nature of the
experience—a connection in the field of consciousness—and
the heightened mental pleasure such moments produce.

> All this fires my soul, and, provided I am not
> disturbed, my subject enlarges itself, becomes
> methodized and defined, and the whole,
> though it be long, stands almost complete
> and finished in my mind, so that I can survey
> it, like a fine picture or a beautiful statue, at a
> glance. Nor do I hear in my imagination the
> parts *successively*, but I hear them, as it were,
> all at once (*gleich alles zusammen*). What a
> delight this is I cannot tell![35].
> **Wolfgang Amadeus Mozart
> —Composer**

> Happy ideas come unexpectedly without
> effort like an inspiration.[36]
> **Hermann Ludwig Helmholtz
> —Physicist**

> I can remember the very spot in the road,
> whilst in my carriage, when to my joy, the
> solution occurred to me.[37]
> **Charles Darwin—Naturalist**

> When I became aware that my mind was
> simmering over something, I had a dim
> feeling which it is very difficult to describe;

it was like a vague impression of mental activity. But when the association had risen to the surface, it expanded into an impression of joy[38].

J. Varendonck—Psycholigist

The idea came like a flash of lightening, and in an instant the truth was revealed... For awhile I gave myself entirely to the intense enjoyment of picturing machines and devising new forms. It was a mental state of happiness about as complete as I have ever known in life.[39]

Nikola Tesla—Inventor

It would be vain to try to put into words that immeasurable sense of bliss which comes over me directly a new idea awakens in me and begins to assume a definite form.[40]

Peter Ilich Tchaikovsky
—Composer

These examples and countless others show that doing less and accomplishing more is indeed subjectively experienced as charm.

In addition, not only is the insight pleasurable but the insight gives pleasure to those who in some way utilize the fruit of that insight. A well-done poem, song, or painting causes pleasure to the reader, listener, viewer because the words or the notes or the colors express so much with so little.

It has been said that art is a tryst; for in the joy of it, maker and beholder meet.[41]

Kojiro Tomita
—Curator, Museum of Fine Arts Boston

The equivalence of charm and doing less and accomplishing more is universal and important because now when we state our consciousness moves in the direction of greater charm, it also means our consciousness moves in the direction of doing less and accomplishing more and this equivalence is vital to our understanding of solutions.

CHAPTER 8

Doing Less and Accomplishing More Is an Expression of Orderliness

Although we are now very close to discovering the secret to solutions, if we are to fully understand how solutions occur, we must explore one more aspect of doing less and accomplishing more and that is: it is not only an objective description of charm, but doing less and accomplishing more is also an objective description of orderliness. This point is important because orderliness is a fundamental aspect of solutions.

Using our example of an automobile engine, we can see how doing less and accomplishing more describes a state of orderliness: any engine that uses a given quantity of gas to propel a car a certain distance is an orderly engine. However, if we fine tune the engine, improve the existing parts, and add new technologies so that the engine uses less gas to propel the car farther, what happens? We increase the orderliness of the engine. And that engine which uses the least amount of gas to propel the car the farthest is the most orderly engine.

Whether it's movies, poetry, music, art, engineering, medicine, architecture, or science doing less and accomplishing more is the goal. Whatever achieves that goal is orderly, and charm, pleasure, and happiness are what we experience when we attain the goal.

Order is one of the needs of life, which when
it is satisfied, produces a real happiness.[42]
Maria Montessori—Educator

In the race of different manufacturers to create the best
electric engine and the best battery to power that engine,
the goal is a product that gets the most mileage, uses the
least amount of energy, requires the shortest recharge time,
and costs the least. Whatever battery and whatever engine
achieve these objectives will be the most orderly battery and
the most orderly engine and will create the most pleasure
for the manufacturer and for all its customers. Orderliness,
doing less and accomplishing more, and pleasure go hand in
hand. Orderliness and doing less and accomplishing more
are two sides of the same coin and pleasure is the subjective
experience of having that coin in our pocket.

Another example of the equivalence of doing less and
accomplishing more, charm, and orderliness is from a movie
called *The Founder*. It's about the beginning of McDonald's,
the famous hamburger chain. At one point in the film,
Michael Keaton who plays Ray Kroc, the founder, is watching
the original McDonald brothers show off their hamburger
restaurant. What's exciting about the restaurant to Kroc is the
remarkable efficiency with which it serves hamburgers. The
original McDonald brothers created a system that does less
and accomplishes more by providing a hamburger, french fries,
and a drink in super-fast time. Of course, the hamburgers also
taste good, and in the movie, we can see how much planning
went into creating the very orderly cooking and serving
process. We can also see the joyous "*ahas*" going off in Ray
Kroc's eyes as he admires the efficiency and the low-cost of this
restaurant and imagines them all over the United States and
the world. Yes, the example is from a movie but does anyone
doubt that McDonald's owes a great deal of its success to the

high level of orderliness with which it produces meal ready food. We can question the goals McDonald's sets for its food and a world where speed and taste are more important than nutritional value but we can't question the efficiency with which McDonald's operates. The tremendous orderliness of its operations is one of the main reasons the restaurant chain causes pleasure to billions of people around the world.

Our consciousness needs orderliness to function and grow and our consciousness produces orderliness everywhere and in every way it can.

> It is amazing how much both happiness and efficiency can be increased by the cultivation of our orderly mind, which thinks about a matter adequately at the right time rather than inadequately at all times.[43]
> **Bertrand Russell—Philosopher**

> Order is the sanity of the mind, the health of the body, the peace of the city, the security of the state. As the beams to a house, as the bones to the body, so is in order to all things.[44]
> **Robert Southey—Poet**

With our senses, we observe the world in an orderly manner. When we see an object, we see it right side up. Matter appears solid. Boundaries are clearly defined. Colors, sounds, and tastes are vivid and distinct. Simply on the level of our perception, every aspect of experiencing is completely systematic and orderly.

When our surroundings are chaotic, our consciousness makes order out of the chaos. If we work in a noisy environment like an airport, our consciousness automatically filters out much of the noise, so that we can communicate with others and get our job done on time. Similarly, if we see a video of scenery shot from inside a moving car, the scenery jumps up and down due to the movement of the car. But if we're actually in the car, our consciousness automatically filters out much of the "jumpiness," permitting us to drive safely without becoming disoriented.

How many times on TV or radio when some event like a riot or a natural disaster strike do we hear the police chief, mayor, or governor (all human symbols of order) say, we must "maintain order?"

Why?

Because human beings require order. The electricity needs to be on, streets need to be cleaned, shops need to be open, and people need to live without fear of violence (disorder).

Order is an innate part of human life from infancy on. Children are raised to create order. In fact, their growth is measured by how well they master order—from controlling the movements of their eyes, heads and limbs, to crawling and walking, to learning to read and write, the accomplishment of which we grade in an orderly way through numbers or letters (A, B, C, D, 4.0, 3.0, 2.0).

> A child is constantly inspecting his surroundings, his 'house'; and when a chair is out of place, making the room look disorderly, we can be certain that it will be the smallest children who will notice it. Before a child reaches the age of three, the highest form of work and the most ennobling that engages him is that of arranging furniture and putting things in order, and it is also the one that calls for the greatest activity.[45]
> **Maria Montessori—Educator**

Human beings spread order everywhere we go. We investigate, catalogue, and categorize everything. From cooking to accounting, from inventing to illustrating, from analyzing to calculating, we attempt to put everything we come into contact with into something systematic and orderly.

> It is the function of science to discover the existence of a general reign of order in nature and to find the causes governing this order. And this refers in equal measure to the relations of man-social and political-and to the entire universe as a whole.[46]
> **Dmitri Ivanovich Mendeleev**
> **—Geneticist**

> The scientist does not study nature because it is useful to do so. He studies it because he takes pleasure in it, and he takes pleasure in it because it is beautiful. If nature were not beautiful it would not be worth knowing, and life would not be worth living. I am not speaking, of course, of the beauty which strikes the senses, of the beauty of qualities and appearances. I am far from despising this, but it has nothing to do with science. What I mean is that more intimate beauty which comes from the harmonious order of its parts, and which a pure intelligence can grasp.[47]
> **Henri Poincaré—Mathematician**

We measure the universe in light years; the earth in miles; the oceans in leagues. Even those things we can't see, we attempt to put into order. Time, that unconquerable tyrant, we attempt to tame by measuring as if with a tailor's tape months, days, hours, and minutes. If that's not enough of a conceit, we establish order in realms beyond time. In religion, we order the heavens, rank angels, and ordain the fate of the soul.

Maimonides, in his Mishneh Torah, counted ten ranks of angels in the Jewish angelic hierarchy, beginning from the highest:

Chayoth Ha Kadesh], Ophanim, Erelim, Hashmallim, Seraphim, Malakim, Elohim, Bene Elohim, Cherubim, Ishim[48]

The most influential Christian angelic hierarchy was that put forward by Pseudo-Dionysius the Areopagite in the 5th or 6th century in his book *De Coelesti Hierarchia* (On the Celestial Hierarchy). Dionysius described nine levels of spiritual beings which he grouped into three orders:

Highest order: Seraphim, Cherubim, Thrones
Middle order: Dominions, Virtues, Powers
Lowest order: Principalities, Archangels,
    Angels[49]

Returning to more earthly realms, we not only establish order in those things most important to us, we establish order in those things that merely amuse us. The games we play have more rules than our work and in "organized" sports we appoint umpires, referees, and commissioners to see that the rules are enforced.

Baseball is about the only orderly thing in a very unorderly world. If you get three strikes even the best lawyer in the world can't get you off.[50]

Bill Veeck—Baseball Owner

One obvious reason Bill Veeck loves sports is because it is so orderly. He does not like it, nor does anyone else, when disorder [injustice] in life occurs.

Through art we bring order to the most refined levels of our intellect and emotions. Every great artist, whether a Michelangelo, Jackson Pollock, Mozart, John Cage, Shakespeare, or Emily Dickinson attempts to incorporate the highest levels of order into his or her art. Techniques and methods might differ. The way the paintings, music, and poetry look, sound, and read might differ but every artist is still attempting to create order. Otherwise, it wouldn't be art. The very act of creating art is the process of expressing beauty, emotion, and meaning through a unique combination of words, color, and/or sound that does less and accomplishes more. Or we can say is one "formal structure in which many elements operate at the same time." Or we can say produces a maximum effect with a minimum of effort. Or we can most simply say is orderly. And, of course, the resulting art always causes pleasure. When a lesser artist puts together notes, words, or colors, he or she might create a pleasant diversion but when a great artist unites the same material, the work vibrates, sparks, explodes. The piece whispers, cries, sings. Why? Words, colors, and notes are the same but when they are assembled by an artist highly skilled at creating unexpected but unexpectedly right (charming) connections, the work conveys the maximum power.

For any work to be art, there has to be a consciousness, an engine of transformation, which takes something less orderly and transforms it into something more orderly. For any artist to accomplish that task, order has to exist within the engine of transformation, i.e., the consciousness of the artist. If the artist's consciousness is unsettled at the time he or she is creating, the unsettled quality of the artist's consciousness is merely moved to a confusion of colors on the canvas. It is only when the artist's consciousness is orderly that the colors on the palette become a disciplined design on the canvas. Whether it is a painting, book, symphony, building, or business the orderliness permeating the creation doesn't come from the creator's hands, eyes, or ears. The orderliness comes from the creator's consciousness:

> 'The mind is the real instrument of sight and observation' and the eyes merely act 'as a kind of vehicle, receiving and transmitting the visual portion of consciousness.' *But the mind is also the real instrument of manual dexterity in a much deeper sense than we generally realize, including those quirks of manner and style which can be 'left to the muscles' to be taken care of.*_Renoir, when his fingers became crippled with arthritis, painted with a brush attached to his forearm, yet his style remained unchanged.[51]
> (emphasis my own)

Even modern, seemingly "chaotic" art is still orderly. Jackson Pollock whose paintings are often criticized as "formless" explains his art this way:

> Technic is the result of a need—
> new needs demand new technics—
> total control—denial of
> the accident—
> States of order—
> organic intensity—
> energy and motion
> made visible—
> memories arrested in space,
> human needs and motives—
> acceptance—[52]

Although Jackson Pollock's style superficially looks "chaotic," chaos is not what Pollock is creating. The *appearance* of chaos is not chaos. His paintings are not random. Even though Pollock's paintings are not portraits or landscapes or any discernible real-life images, Pollock's paintings are still composed. His pictures display unique patterns and shapes, harmonies and rhythms. In his own words, Pollock's paintings are attempts to "make visible energy and motion," and in those attempts, Pollock is in "total control," "denies the accident," and is creating "states of order." What we see when we gaze at Pollock's works and why they hang in museums around the world is not a misplaced reverence for dribbles of color and indiscernible design. Pollock's painting are precise and purposeful. Each drop of paint belongs. Each drop of paint is exactly the right color, width, and thickness. Each drop of paint is in exactly the right place and each drop of paint spontaneously, naturally, and innocently expresses complete order because we cannot alter one drop, color, or shape without making his pictures less perfect.

> Pollock's superiority to his contemporaries in this country lies in his ability to create a genuinely violent and extravagant art without losing stylistic control.[53]
> **Clement Greenberg—Art Critic**

You might wonder how Pollock's paint strokes can be said to be under control since he is famous for his "dribble" or "splash" techniques. But the answer is very simple. How do Leonardo da Vinci, Rembrandt, and Botticelli paint? They take their brush, dip it into some paint, and apply it to the canvas. Then, they step back and see how the brush stroke looks. If it is correct, they leave it, and go on to the next stroke. If it's incorrect, they modify it or paint over it and they keep repeating the process until the painting is complete.

How does Jackson Pollock work? The exact same way. He takes his brush or stick, dips it into some paint, and then he drips or splashes the paint on the canvas. Then, just like da Vinci, Rembrandt, and Botticelli, he steps back and examines what he's done. If the strokes—the splashes or dribbles—are what he likes, he goes on to another part of the canvas. If they are not what he likes, he makes another splash or dribble in the same area until the splashes or dribbles are exactly where he wants them. Like da Vinci, Rembrandt, and Botticelli, he then goes on to another part of the canvas until the painting is complete, until the painting looks exactly how he, Pollock, wants it, until every drop or splash of paint is exactly where it belongs.

Even though it is clear from this explanation that the process is the same and it is a process of increasing orderliness, we still might stubbornly disagree because it is hard to accept the dribbles and splashes as having "intent." There's that expression that has grown up around the paintings of Pollock: "My kid could do that." Well, you or your kids try it and see what you end up with and then compare it to a Jackson Pollock. This exercise doesn't mean you can't create something great but rather that you will find that there is much more "intent" involved.

Every work of art (or whatever we as humans produce) is a direct expression of our consciousness. Even an artist like Van Gogh, whose life in many ways was severely troubled doesn't mean that his consciousness—at least when he was painting—was disorderly. No matter what was going on in Van Gogh's life, his consciousness when he was creating was in a highly alert and coherent state.

In letters to his brother, Van Gogh describes his mental state when he is painting:

> These colors give me extraordinary exaltation.
> I have no thought of fatigue; I shall do another
> picture this very night, and I shall bring it
> off. *I have a terrible lucidity at moments when
> nature is so beautiful...*[54] (emphasis my own)

And again:

> ...if these emotions are sometimes so strong
> that we work without being aware that we
> are working, *if sometimes the brush strokes
> come in sequence and inter-relation like
> words in a speech or a letter*, then we must
> remember that it is not always like that, and
> that there are going to be hard days without
> inspiration...[55] (emphasis my own)

From these quotes, we can see that Van Gogh works best
when his consciousness is clearest (has a "terrible lucidity"),
and is most orderly ("brush strokes come in sequence and
inter-relation"). What makes Van Gogh (or any artist) great
is not, as many people believe, the suffering (disorder) he
endured. Suffering (disorder) is never a source of creativity
because creativity requires energy (creativity) and intelligence
(discrimination, decision making) which are *always* at their
height when our consciousness is clearest and most coherent.
When Van Gogh suffered, his consciousness was disorderly
and incapable of creativity. That is when his "days were hard
and without inspiration." That is when Van Gogh could
barely think or act, never mind paint works which display
the highest levels of truth, originality, and beauty.

In the letter below, we see Van Gogh clinging desperately
to whatever shred of tranquility exists in his life, so that he
can continue painting:

I hope it will be sufficient if I say that I feel definitely incapable of starting all over again with the hiring of a studio and living in it alone; whether it be here in Arles or anywhere else comes to the same thing at the moment. I have tried to get used to the idea of a fresh start, but it is impossible for the moment.

I should be afraid of losing the *capacity to work, which is at present returning, if I forced myself to keep a studio, with all the other responsibilities involved.*

And for the present I wish to remain in confinement, for my own peace of mind as well as for that of others.[56] (emphasis my own)

What Van Gogh desires to continue painting is "peace of mind", not suffering. In the lives of many great artists, many of whom endure great pain, we can see that, while their suffering may influence their art and be expressed in their art, at the time that they are actually *engaged* in their art, their consciousness is orderly. Indeed, their art is often the only positive part of their lives and the sole refuge into which they retreat for spiritual and mental sustenance, because of the very peace (orderliness, pleasure, charm, calmness) that the process of creating brings. Again, from Van Gogh:

The doctor has given me strict orders to go out to walk without doing any mental work, but work distracts me, and I *must* have some distraction; *or rather work keeps me in control, so that I don't deny myself it.* (emphasis my own)[57]

While suffering might bring artists to the solace of their art and be reflected in their art, it is not the *source of their ability to create.* For artists to create, their consciousness at the time they are creating must be orderly. Order can only emerge from order. Order cannot emerge from chaos and great art is highly ordered. As we can see from the quotes of Van Gogh, art both is created by an orderly consciousness and helps the artist's consciousness gain order.

Since we are talking a lot about order, we might wonder where chaos fits in and why there is so much of it in our own life and in the world. First, in the broadest sense, we can say chaos does not exist. When people use the term "chaos" to describe a tornado, a volcano, an earthquake, an exploding star, or a pile of junk, we are really not talking about chaos. Everything on earth, just like everything in the universe, consists of particles and motions which follow precise, determinable, measurable, and orderly laws. Always. Eternally. Immutably. We term some events or processes chaotic when A: we lack the knowledge to explain and/or predict the actions taking place; or B: when one orderly system disrupts the orderliness of another system.

> From where we stand the rain seems random. If we could stand somewhere else, we would see the order in it.[58]
> **Tony Hillerman—Author**

> Chaos is merely order waiting to be deciphered.[59]
> **José Saramago—Author**

> There is order and even great beauty in what looks like total chaos. If we look closely enough at the randomness around us, patterns will start to emerge.[60]
> **Aaron Sorkin**
> **—Scriptwriter and Producer**

Some systems like an earthquake or a snow storm have so many variables it makes them difficult or impossible to predict, but it is not because the system does not behave according to the orderly laws of physics.

Many scientists today study these "chaotic" systems and are better able to accurately calculate their outcomes.

> Mathematicians are beginning to discover the algorithms underlying "chaotic" systems and these algorithms are surprisingly simple and orderly and yet give rise to very complex patterns. And more systems previously viewed as "chaotic" are now understandable and predictable and thus more orderly.[61]
>
> **James Gleick—Author**

"Chaotic" is also a term we frequently ascribe to certain human behavior like wars, murders, and terrorism. But even here, when we search deeply enough, we find order (a motive). The motive might be as twisted as the behavior but it is there. We might say that a dictator, murderer, or terrorist was insane but in the consciousness of the perpetrator, the behavior makes sense. And there is order in the way the terror is planned and carried out. The terrorists build their bombs, buy their guns, and recruit others to assist them. They are like a disease that threatens a larger system and has to be eliminated, but the disease itself has its own rules. A human being is a highly ordered system but a virus or a bacteria, which are also orderly systems, can cause havoc to the order within the human being. Or an invading army, which is an orderly system, can destroy another orderly system i.e., the country it invades. Or a bulldozer, which is an orderly machine, can reduce a house to rubble. All of which, again, illustrates that order is everywhere, even in chaos.

It is interesting to note that some people love horror movies and scary books, which seems to belie the desire for or love of order. But even horror movies, plays, and books have order. They emerge from out of the orderly "*aha*" experiences of their authors and screenwriters and require order in every aspect of their creation. Just as comedies and dramas have their own structure, horror movies, plays, and books do as well. Writers, directors, and actors operate within artistic "horror" conventions to orchestrate the emotions of their audiences to provide the maximum horror, i.e., do the least to accomplish the most. And, in their endings, when the horror and the fear ends, they do produce some level of order in the consciousness of their audience.

Alfred Hitchcock, the great director, who is known as the master of suspense, explains one of the film techniques he uses this way:

> There is a difference between "suspense" and "surprise," and yet many pictures continually confuse the two. I'll explain what I mean.
>
> We are now having a very innocent little chat. Let us suppose that there is a bomb underneath this table between us. Nothing happens and then all of a sudden, "Boom!" There is an explosion. The public is *surprised* but prior to this surprise, it has seen an absolutely ordinary scene, of no special consequence. Now, let us take a suspense situation. The bomb is underneath the table and the public *knows* it, probably because they have seen the anarchist place it there. The public is *aware* that the bomb is going to explode at one o'clock and there is a clock in the décor. The public can see that it is a

quarter to one. In these conditions this same innocuous conversation becomes fascinating because the public is participating in the scene. The audience is longing to warn the characters in the scene: "You shouldn't be talking about such trivial matters. There's a bomb beneath you and it's about to explode!"

In the first case we have given the public fifteen seconds of *surprise* at the moment of the explosion. In the second case we have provided them with fifteen minutes of *suspense*. The conclusion is that whenever possible the public must be informed...."[62]

Knowing this technique of suspense, remember the horror movies we've seen. When a girl is walking home at night alone in a well-directed horror movie, we always see the man with the knife in the clown/hockey/bunny mask, hiding behind the bushes. Once we know that the killer is there, it makes every step the girl takes more terrifying. That the single camera shot of the man in the mask hiding behind the bushes adds such intense feelings throughout the girl's walk is just one example of how, even in horror movies, the art is accomplishing more by doing less.

At the beginning of a horror movie from the comfort of our theater seat or living room couch, we, as audience members, voluntarily surrender to the chaos of the film because it's temporary, fake, and resolved by the ending when the murderer/monster is slain or at least temporarily vanquished (until the sequel). And what's also important, the motive for the mayhem is also explained. For example, in *Psycho,* near the end of the movie, Alfred Hitchcock devotes four minutes of valuable film time to have an actor/psychiatrist explain the reason Norman Bates (Anthony Perkins) murders, which demonstrates how important Hitchcock feels a return to a rational universe is for the audience. Now whether or not the explanation of multiple personalities, etc. is psychologically valid is irrelevant. It is enough that the audience accepts it, so that what seemed random and chaotic becomes orderly and clear and the audience leaves the theater, feeling some resolution and enjoys the (hopefully) higher orderliness of their own lives.

One of the more counterintuitive findings in the science of fear is that the stronger the negative emotions (fear, worry, anxiety...) a person reports experiencing during horror films, the more likely he or she is to enjoy the genre. Distress and delight are correlated. "The pleasure comes from the relief that follows," says Campbell. "It provides a cathartic effect, offering you emotional release and escape from the real world of bills and mortgages and the economy and relationships."[63]

Sharon Begley—Writer

It's not that we like sad movies that make us feel like, 'Oh, my God, what a bummer.' We like emotionally moving experiences. It's nothing new. It's catharsis. It goes back to the Greeks.[64]

Gayle Forman—Writer

Being scared by a movie offers a safe catharsis, because the terror is confined to the screen. It's an adrenalin spike, and when I come back down, I feel a bit more leveled.[65]

Laura van den Berg—Writer

Human beings are capable of experiencing many emotions and art, in particular "story" art, whether it be written or performed, provides an individual with the pleasure of wide swings of emotions, all while knowing that no one is actually hurt, that the problems presented will in some way be resolved and, in any event, aren't real. All these "safety nets" make drama and its extreme step-sister, horror, pleasurable. It is chaos contained within the boundaries of order—the orderliness of the movie, play, or book and the orderliness of our own lives which in comparison to the havoc conveyed in the movie, play, or book is always better and thus makes us feel "more levelled" when we return to our own skin.

One final fact that reinforces the truth that desire for order, charm, and enjoyment holds throughout all our lives and certainly in the books we read and the plays and movies we see is that no one voluntarily watches or reads what they dislike. If we like horror movies, we "like" horror movies for whatever reason. And for those of us who like horror movies, we like best the movies, plays, or books that produce their horror with the most skill—do less and accomplish more—in whatever genre of horror we like. Pleasure (orderliness, doing less and accomplishing more) always pervades our choices.

CHAPTER 9

Disorder and Order

We have talked a lot about order and disorder, however, in this chapter, we shall see that, paradoxically, the two forces are not antithetical but are actually complementary. Strangely enough, nature needs order *and* disorder. In fact, if we look into the very heart of order, *we see a certain inherent disorder exists within its core.*

Look at our most orderly state: pure consciousness. We've seen how pure consciousness by virtue of its own nature—awareness—inevitably "breaks;" that pure consciousness becomes aware of itself and that this self-awareness causes consciousness to become three—the observer, the object observed, and the act of observing. This phenomenon is an inevitable and inseparable aspect of consciousness and it demonstrates that the most stable aspect of ourself—pure consciousness—by virtue of its own nature—awareness—is also the most unstable. By its very nature awareness must "break," must become aware of itself, which means that "disorder" is an inevitable part of order.

While this example is abstract, the reality of disorder existing within order can be demonstrated in more concrete ways. From the tiniest sub-atomic particles to the largest galaxies, the material world is always dissolving, separating, and reuniting. The material world, which we think of as very solid, is actually the flimsiest, most changeable, most impermanent, evanescent stuff ever conceived. Transformation is its only constant. Galaxies, stars, and planets appear and disappear. Humans, animals, and plants are born and die. Nothing lasts. Everything winks in and out of existence. From the very large to the very small.

> Even in a perfect vacuum, pairs of virtual particles are constantly being created and destroyed.[66]
> **Richard Morris—Author**

> "New" atoms are incorporated into our bodies at every moment, and "old" ones are rearranged, while some are pushed out. Every few days we essentially recycle ourselves, reminiscent of an old advertising jingle for milk, "There's a new you coming every day!" Except it's more like every hour, minute, second, instant.[67]
> **David P. Barash—Author**

> Main sequence stars over eight solar masses are destined to die in a titanic explosion called a supernova. A supernova is not merely a bigger nova. In a nova, only the star's surface explodes. In a supernova, the star's core collapses and then explodes. In massive stars, a complex series of nuclear reactions leads to the production of iron in the core. Having achieved iron, the star has wrung all the energy it can out of nuclear fusion—fusion reactions that form elements heavier than iron actually consume energy rather than produce it. The star no longer has any way to support its own mass, and the iron collapses. In just a matter of seconds

the core shrinks from roughly 5000 miles across to just a dozen, and the temperature spikes 100 billion degrees or more. The outer layers of the star initially begin to collapse along with the core, but rebound with the enormous release of energy and are thrown violently outward. Supernovae release an almost unimaginable amount of energy. For a period of days to weeks, a supernovae may outshine an entire galaxy. Likewise, all the naturally occurring elements and a rich array of subatomic particles are produced in these explosions. On average, a supernovae explosion occurs about once every hundred years in the typical galaxy. About 25 to 50 supernovae are discovered each year in other galaxies, but most are too far away to be seen without a telescope.[68]

Destruction is part of life in the Universe. Without destruction everything remains in the status quo and fails to progress. To survive, we eat plants and animals. To make furniture, we chop down trees. To drive cars, we drill for oil (or even in the case of electric cars, we mine for the rare minerals that are required for the batteries). Simply to walk, one foot abandons its present position and moves forward and establishes a new position which in turn is abandoned.

All the above proves an old adage—you can't make an omelet without breaking eggs. Creation needs disorder to function. Order and disorder are the necessary steps of creation. Disorder even exists within our definition of order: doing less and accomplishing more. The desire to do less conflicts with the desire to accomplish more. Yet, these two opposing forces when working together produce higher and higher states of order.

As in our example of an engine—due to our desire to accomplish more, we expend energy to modify the engine (disorder). But due to our desire to do less, we improve the efficiency of the engine, which now gets more mileage with less fuel (a higher state of order). However, since our desire to accomplish more never ceases, we expend more energy, modifying the current engine (disorder) to improve its efficiency (a higher state of order) and so on.

Or if we look at our own engine of transformation, our consciousness, due to our desire to accomplish more, we expend energy to alter (disorder) our current mental state, perhaps, to study algebra (this is a math example but it could be any discipline or field). But due to our desire to do less, once we learn algebra, we produce a more capable and efficient mental state (a higher state of order). But due to our consciousness' unquenchable desire to accomplish more, we modify (disorder) our present mental state, expending another bit of energy to study trigonometry, and we gain a more efficient mental state (a higher state of order). Then we study calculus. Then we study differential equations. Then we study linear algebra and so on in a continual cycle of progress brought about by the opposing forces within order—the desire to accomplish more and the desire to do less. When these two opposing forces interact, they always flow toward more orderliness, more charm, and as, at last, we shall see, more solutions.

CHAPTER 10

Our Consciousness Is a Solution System

An intimate connection exists between order and solutions. In fact, the relationship between order and solutions is so intimate, we can define a solution as any act, concept, or process which increases the orderliness of a system.

When an artist paints a picture, the empty, blank canvas is the orderliness of emptiness. With the application of the first brush stroke, the artist begins the process of painting, working on the canvas as it passes through various stages of order and disorder. Each brush stroke presents the artist with new problems—difficulties of balance, theme, color, and proportion—until the last brush stroke solves the last problem and provides the painting with its highest level of orderliness: that level which does the least and accomplishes the most; which expresses the most beauty, produces the most charm: the orderliness of fullness—the successful solution to all the problems the painting presented.

Or when a businessman starts a business, he begins with his empty factory, store, cash register, and as he develops his business—searching for the right product, the right way to make it, and the right way to sell it—his business passes through increasing levels of order and disorder until his business arrives at the highest level of orderliness and charm. It is at this highest level that the business does the least, yet accomplishes the most i. e., makes the best product at the lowest cost, pleases the most customers, and earns the highest profit. Another orderliness of fullness; another completed solution to all of the business' problems.

Or when a scientist searches for a discovery, the scientist begins with the orderliness of emptiness—a blank notebook, sterile instruments, and a clean lab—and as the scientist attempts experiment after experiment, test after test, calculation after calculation, trying to uncover new laws of nature and new ways to use them, the scientist's research passes through progressive stages of order and disorder until eventually he or she arrives at the highest level of orderliness and charm. And it is again at this highest level that we have the finished discovery—the formula, invention, or theory that explains the most in the simplest way or cures the most people in the safest way or travels the farthest or the fastest, using the least amount of energy, and is again the orderliness of fullness and the successful solution to all the problems posed by the scientist's quest.

Therefore, we can say a solution not only increases the orderliness, efficiency, and charm of a system but is the final connection, the master stroke, the ultimate *"aha"* that completes it—that beyond anything else allows a system to fulfill its function doing the least and accomplishing the most.

Except we still haven't revealed where *"ahas"* come from. What the mysterious process is by which ideas, inspirations, and connections occur? What makes an illumination moment happen?

However, finally, having analyzed consciousness in detail, we have the knowledge to arrive at the answer. When we review the principles that make up the nature of consciousness, they lead us to one conclusion—because solutions increase the orderliness of a system by doing the least and accomplishing the most; because the subjective experience of doing the least and accomplishing the most is charm; because consciousness moves naturally, spontaneously, and effortlessly in the direction of greater charm; and because consciousness moves in the direction of greater charm *by itself, consciousness moves in the direction of solutions on its own!*

In other words, our consciousness is our solution system. It is as natural for our consciousness to create solutions as it is for water to flow downhill.

While the world goes mad trying to improve problem solving through better schools, libraries, computers, cell phones, and labs, it ignores the most important resource we have—our own consciousness. Despite how difficult solving problems sometimes seems, despite the number of problems that exist in the world, despite the turmoil that often dominates our mind, our consciousness is endowed with the inherent ability to solve problems simply, spontaneously, and effortlessly because solving problems *is its nature.*

We provide our consciousness with the information to solve a problem. We provide our consciousness with the desire to solve a problem but **it is the nature of consciousness itself to make the connections which are the solution.** In fact, our consciousness solves problems so naturally, effortlessly, and spontaneously, we only become aware that our consciousness has solved a problem *after* the problem is solved. *After* our consciousness has selected, organized, and connected disparate pieces of information into a new and useful sequence which is our solution. That's when we say, "aha." That's when we say, "Eureka." That's when we say, "I've got it." It's our own consciousness which gives us the solution.

From a field of incoherence which is a problem (less creativity, less intelligence, less orderliness, less charm), our consciousness arranges, organizes, and connects the data into a field of coherence (greater charm, greater creativity, greater intelligence, greater orderliness) that is our solution. And because the movement of consciousness in the direction of greater charm occurs due to our consciousness' own nature, we only realize the solution *after* it appears!

When we strain, when we control, when we force, we interfere with our consciousness' natural ability to function as a solution system. When we let our consciousness alone, when we stop trying, when we take a break, when we let our consciousness function freely on its own, that's when, suddenly, the right idea dawns. Indeed, whatever simple mental tricks many of us employ for solving problems such as taking a walk or going for a drive or putting off the problem until the next day (when we've had a good night's sleep) are based on this common experience that our consciousness works best when it is *fresh, clear, and free.*

The reason why the "aha" experience seems so magical and mysterious is because the answer to problems well up spontaneously from deep within. We are struggling with a problem—we are trying this way and that—and then after, perhaps, hours of frustration, we stop struggling and stare out the window or go to the kitchen for a snack and POP! the answer appears. Why? Because our consciousness is a solution system and solutions—when they occur—always occur naturally, effortlessly, and spontaneously due to the nature of consciousness to move in the direction of greater charm—our *"aha"—by itself.*

Common phrases like "out of the blue," "as if by magic," "from out of nowhere," "in a flash," are all expressions used over the centuries to describe the exact moment the phenomenon of a solution occurs and *each phrase clearly implies that the moment of solution is not laborious or forced. The moment of solution naturally, innocently, and effortlessly comes to us.*

> Often when one works at a hard question, nothing good is accomplished in the first attack. Then one takes a rest, longer or

shorter, and sits down anew to the work. During the first half-hour, as before, nothing is found, and then all of a sudden the decisive idea presents itself to the mind.[69]

Henri Poincare—Mathematician

Sitting and trying to force an idea to come is not a good thing to do. Sometimes, you just want to get out and change your brain, have some fun. Sometimes, we do the most creative things playing, or taking a shower in the morning.[70]

Gianfranco Zaccai—Designer

Inability to relax, to let go of a problem, often prevents its solution.[71]

Eugene Raudsepp
—Author and Researcher

While daydreaming, the brain enters an alpha wave state, a more relaxed state of mind. This calm and slightly detached state, which is the hallmark of daydreaming, helps to "quiet the noise" so that we can experience the answer or connection.

What's weird is that the moment of insight seems to happen before we're even consciously aware of it, according to the study. That's why the answer seems to come out of nowhere.[72]

Amy Fries—Writer

Every code breaker had his or her method of coping with frustration. Frank Rowlett liked to go to bed early, then wake up in the middle of the night and see if inspiration struck him.[73]

Liza Mundy—Author

After all, most writing is done away from the typewriter, away from the desk. I'd say it occurs in the quiet, silent moments, while you're walking or shaving or playing a game, or whatever, or even talking to someone you're not really interested in.[74]

Henry Miller—Writer

When problems don't work well, I always go home with them and I sort of tuck them away and then I'll catch an idea when I'm shaving or something of this sort.[75]

Paul Saltman—Chemist

Ideas, I find, come most readily when you are doing something that keeps the mind alert without putting too much strain on it. Shaving, driving a car, sawing a plank, or fishing or hunting, for instance. Or engaging with some friend in stimulating conversation.[76]

Lenox Riley Lohr—Businessman

Why do I always find my best ideas while shaving?[77]

Albert Einstein—Physicist

The initial inspiration, which is the most interesting, in a way, usually comes when you're not trying to do something. The more relaxed you are, the more fun you're having, and the more you're just not trying—that's when you get your initial inspiration.[78]

**Mick Jagger
—Musician and Songwriter**

These common experiences are why, when we have a solution, we are so exhilarated because of the joy of it and yet so humble because of the inner sense that it is not our small individual, struggling self that reaches a solution. In some extraordinary, inexplicable way the solution, *like a gift from nature,* comes to us.

In ancient times it was the tradition of artists, writers, poets, and philosophers to delegate responsibility for this "gift" not to themselves but to some higher being—some god or goddess to whom they prayed for continued aid. The Greeks in their penchant for systemization named nine specific muses of the arts: Calliope for epic poetry and eloquence; Euterpe for music and lyric poetry; Erato for love poetry; Polyhymnia for oratory or sacred poetry; Clio for history; Melpomene for tragedy; Thalia for comedy; Terpsichore for choral singing and dance; and Urania for astronomy.[79]

Plato, in his dialogue, ION, clearly states he sees "solutions" as coming from these muses:

> Many are the noble words in which poets speak concerning the actions of men; but like yourself when speaking about Homer, they do not speak of them by any rules of art: they are simply inspired to utter that to which the Muse impels them, and that only...for not by art does the poet sing, but by power divine.[80]

Ancient dramatic and poetic works, whether Greek or otherwise, often include a prayer to a higher being, pleading for assistance during those periods of terrible helplessness we all endure when we are looking for a solution.

> O light supreme, who so far dost uplift
> thee over mortal thoughts, lend again to

my mind a little of what thou didst seem
and give my tongue such power that it may
leave a single sparkle of thy glory to
future men…[81]

Dante—Poet

Sing in me Muse, and through me tell the story
of that man skilled in all ways of contending,
the wandered, harried for years on end,
after he plundered the stronghold
on the proud height of Troy.[82]

The Odyssey—Homer

Sing Heav'nly Muse, that on the secret top
Of *Oreb*, or of *Sinai*, didst inspire
That Shepherd, who first taught the chosen
     Seed,
In the Beginning how the Heav'ns and Earth
Rose out of *Chaos*: or if *Sion* Hill
Delight thee more, and *Siloa's* brook that flow'd
Fast by the Oracle of God; I thence
Invoke thy aid to my adventurous Song
That with no middle flight intends to soar
Above th' *Aonian* Mount, while it pursues
Things unattempted yet in Prose or Rhime.[83]

John Milton—Poet

And even modern artists pay occasional (if somewhat
amused) homage to the heavenly muses.

> I said to Mrs. Arlen… "Let's go to Grauman's
> Chinese…you drive the car. I don't feel too
> well right now." I wasn't thinking of work…
> I just wanted to relax. And as we drove by
> Schwab's Drugstore on Sunset I said, "Pull
> over, please." And we stopped and really
> don't know why—bless the muses—and I

took out my little bit of manuscript and put down what you know as *Over the Rainbow*.[84]
Harold Arlen—Composer

The composer starts with his theme; and the theme is a gift from Heaven. He doesn't know where it comes from—has no control over it. It comes almost like automatic writing. That's why he keeps a book very often and writes themes down whenever they come. He collects musical ideas. You can't do anything about that element of composing.[85]
Aaron Copeland—Composer

However, as we now understand, the process of inspiration is not a miracle. It's not a mystery. It's not a favor from the gods. Solutions are due to the natural functioning of our own consciousness when we let it operate on its own.

It is the creativity (energy) and intelligence (discrimination) within consciousness which allows it to move naturally, effortlessly, and spontaneously in the direction of doing less and accomplishing more, orderliness, and charm. It is when this experience occurs that solutions pop up and is why the experience seems like a gift—but it is not a gift. It is our own consciousness behaving as what it is—a solution system.

I went to bed that night as usual, and slept, according to my wont, quite soundly. I awoke in the gray of the morning twilight; and as I lay waiting for the dawn, the long lines of the desired poem began to twine themselves in my mind. Having thought out all the stanzas, I said to myself, "I must get up and write these verses down, lest I fall asleep again and forget them." So, with a sudden effort, I sprang out of bed, and found in the dimness an old stump of a pencil which I remembered to have used the day before. I scrawled the verses almost without looking at the paper.[86]

Julia Ward Howe—Poet and Author

However, having reached this point where we've discovered that if our consciousness is a solution system and solving problems is an inherent ability of it, why is it so common to struggle with problems? Why can we be stuck for hours, days, weeks, and years, trying to find a solution? If our consciousness is a solution system, why do we not function as a solution system all the time? Why are we sometimes better at solving problems and sometimes worse? Sometimes much worse?

The answer is because our consciousness is not in a fixed state. From morning to night, from day to day, from week to week, from month to month, our consciousness changes. Sometimes our consciousness is fresh and clear. Sometimes our consciousness is confused and foggy. Sometimes our consciousness is calm and content. Sometimes our consciousness is anxious and chaotic. And sometimes we just don't know enough. We lack the information.

Our consciousness is a solution system but it requires very specific qualities to be in a solution state. When all these qualities are present to the sufficient degree, our consciousness, like a cosmic spider, naturally and effortlessly spins profound and wondrous solutions out of itself.

CHAPTER 11

The Specific Qualities Necessary for Consciousness to Solve Problems

What are the specific qualities our consciousness requires to function as a solution system?

This question is easily answered because our consciousness needs just seven qualities, six of which are inherent aspects of consciousness and the seventh is information, which we should all recognize as an element necessary for solutions.

The seven qualities are: alertness, creativity (energy), intelligence (discrimination, direction), orderliness, freedom from mental control or effort, information, and desire.

When these seven elements are present to the sufficient degree (when we are awake, they are always present to some degree), our consciousness operates as a solution system. When one or more of these qualities is not present to the sufficient degree, our consciousness still behaves as a solution system—that is what it is—but its ability to solve problems is diminished.

"*Aha*s," like hats, come in all shapes and sizes. It could be we're driving and want to figure out the shortest route home; or we're in the kitchen, deciding on the best ingredients for a meal; or we're at the office, dealing with a marketing problem; or we're in a lab, trying to discover the perfect artificial sugar. But wherever we are, whatever we're engaged in, our consciousness is the foundation for solving problems and, the more difficult the problem, the more of the seven qualities required for solutions we need.

Alertness is the primary quality necessary for solutions. If our consciousness is not awake, all the qualities inherent within consciousness are shut down and the entire process by which solutions occur does not take place. With the onset of alertness, our consciousness becomes active. All the qualities of consciousness become lively. Alertness even enhances information. If the data is in our brain, heightened alertness can make the information easier to access. The greater our alertness, the greater the power of our consciousness to organize and combine our thoughts into the best solution. No matter what task we're performing, we always do it better the wider awake we are.

Creativity (energy), is the second quality required for solutions. When our consciousness has energy, it moves. It flows. And since it is through the flow of our consciousness in the direction of greater charm we arrive at solutions, it is vital that our consciousness has the energy to move. The more capable our consciousness is of movement, the greater our potential for solutions (of course, we are not talking about wildness and runaway thoughts).

Intelligence is the third quality. If the movement of consciousness is to be in the direction of greater charm (i.e., the direction of doing less and accomplishing more, i.e., the direction of orderliness), our consciousness must have intelligence. The more precisely our consciousness can discriminate between various choices, the greater is its ability to flow in the direction of greater charm—our *"aha"*.

Orderliness is the fourth quality required for solutions. If our consciousness is orderly, it correctly organizes and interprets data. In a field of order, everything easily connects.

Consciousness has the potential to flow in any direction and does not need a large amount of energy to move. In a field of orderliness, our intelligence can discern differences clearly. In a field of disorder, it is very difficult to connect anything. Expressions like, "I was running around like a chicken *without its head*," says it all. When we are "without a head," obviously we have very little intelligence. Maybe we have energy but our decision-making is weak and confused, and a weak and confused consciousness is not going to connect data easily or correctly. When our consciousness is overwhelmed by anxiety, anger, or fear, our thoughts scatter every which way and we cannot make the connections that create solutions.

Imagine a person in a boat in the middle of the sea. If the sea is calm, the boat easily moves in any direction. Think of the same boat in a storm. The boat's movements are restricted. It's tossed by the waves, blown by the wind. Similarly, if our consciousness is tumultuous, our thoughts swirl and we see obstacles where none exist. Such a mental state is not the best environment for solutions.

Previously we have discussed that disorder is an inherent part of order and necessary for solutions. It is how nature progresses. However, it is not the disorder that overwhelms the system and renders it useless. It is a disorder that is a step in the creative process. It is the disorder that serves as the catalyst for further growth; the disorder within a highly ordered system; the speck of sand in the oyster that creates the pearl.

Another important point: when we talk of orderliness (and in this book we talk of orderliness often), *we do not mean rigidity and restrictedness. We mean a natural orderliness.* Orderliness is frequently mistaken for narrowness and inflexibility like soldiers marching in a straight line. But rigidity, narrowness, and inflexibility have no place in our definition of order. Narrowness, rigidity, and inflexibility prevent the flow of consciousness and limit the range of thought.

With rigidity, our consciousness moves in predictable patterns that have already been tried and proved devoid of answers. When we are rigid, inflexible, and narrow, it hinders our consciousness from the consideration of the new, the untried, and the unusual, which are the lifeblood of solutions. Narrowness, rigidity, and inflexibility produce resistance. Our consciousness may want to flow in one direction but we are too rigid to let it. When we think of the greatest solutions, they come from a consciousness combining information in new and original ways. They are examples of unrestricted thinking. Seeing problems from new angles. Orderly but unrestricted. Orderly but fluid. An orderliness derived from naturalness, innocence, and spontaneity.

Delight in Disorder

> A sweet disorder in the dress
> Kindles in clothes, a wantonness
> A lawn about the shoulders' thrown
> Into a fine distraction
> An erring lace, which here and there
> Enthralls the crimson stomacher
> A cuff neglectful, and thereby
> Ribbons to flow confusedly
> A winning wave, deserving note
> In the tempestuous petticoat
> A careless shoestring, in whose tie
> I see a wild civility
> More bewitch me than when art
> Is too precise in every part[87]
> **Robert Herrick—Poet**

Orderliness and freedom may not seem like qualities that go together, but true orderliness cannot exist without freedom, and true freedom cannot exist without orderliness, which is why freedom is our fifth element required for solutions. Chaos that overwhelms a system is NOT freedom. Freedom is not random motion. Chaos is the prison of its own inability to move intelligently. If our consciousness is to create better and better solutions, it must have the freedom to select, to distinguish, to choose from the widest range of options. That range and fineness of choice can only be made from a platform of stability, calmness, and coherence (orderliness). When a ballerina pirouettes across a stage, a pianist ripples his fingers across a keyboard, or a basketball player slam-dunks a ball, it is a freedom born of long years of study, practice, and discipline (orderliness). Study, practice, and discipline instill in our consciousness and our body the mental and physical knowledge that provide us with the foundation for freedom.

> The beautiful thing in classical ballet is the preparation. To begin with one simple step and to build from there requires endless hours of training, creating, rehearsals, and repetition. Eventually, the choreography begins to take shape and the steps become your own. Then you are able to "let go" and feel free during the performance because by that time, the hard part is over.[88]
> **Olivier Wecxsteen—Dancer**

> Creativity arises out of the tension between spontaneity and limitations, the latter (like the river banks) forcing the spontaneity into the various forms which are essential to the work of art or poem.[89]
> **Rollo May—Author**

> Sometimes restrictions get the mind going. If you've got tons and tons of money, you may relax and figure you can throw money at any problem that comes along. You don't

have to think so hard. But when you have limitations, sometimes you come up with very creative, inexpensive ideas.[90]

David Lynch—Filmmaker

It may sound like a contradiction, but you achieve spontaneity on the set through preparation of the dialogue at home.[91]

Michael Caine—Actor

Freedom is moving easy in harness.[92]

Robert Frost—Poet

Effective performance is preceded by painstaking preparation.

**Brian Tracy
—Author, Motivational Speaker**

No matter what the subject may be, there is only one course for the beginner; he must at first accept a discipline imposed from without, but only as a means of obtaining freedom for, and strengthening himself in, his own method of expression...[93] The need for restriction, for deliberately submitting to a style, has its source in the very depths of our nature, and is found not only in matters of art, but in every conscious manifestation of human activity. It is the need for order without which nothing can be achieved, and upon the disappearance of which everything disintegrates. Now all order demands constraint. But one would be wrong to regard that as any impediment to liberty. On the contrary, the style, the restraint, contribute to its development, and only prevent liberty from degenerating into license.[94]

Igor Stravinski—Composer

> To let the child do as he likes when he has
> not yet developed any powers of control is to
> betray the idea of freedom.[95]
>   **Maria Montessori—Educator**

Van Gogh studied painting from art schools and from other artists, learning the fundamentals of color, proportion, composition, and anatomy. Yet his study did not prevent Van Gogh from breaking conventional forms and creating highly original and revolutionary art. Yet, even while veering far from conventional forms, Van Gogh's art still displays the highest degrees of harmony, structure, balance, and order.

> *Starry Night* is often considered to be Van Gogh's pinnacle achievement. …Here, Van Gogh followed a strict principal of structure and composition in which the forms are distributed across the surface of the canvas in an exact order to create balance and tension amidst the swirling torsion of the cypress trees and the night sky. The result is a landscape rendered through curves and lines, its seeming chaos subverted by a rigorous formal arrangement. Evocative of the spirituality Van Gogh found in nature, *Starry Night* is famous for advancing the act of painting beyond the representation of the physical world.[96]

Thus, Van Gogh could paint stormy and violent scenes but it was always within an orderly structure. And, in those moments when he actually took up his brush, even if his art was depicting stormy and violent emotions, he had sufficient mental clarity and calmness to accomplish the task. Why? Because for an artist to produce great art (and Van Gogh produced much art that is great), it requires in the consciousness of the artist, *at the time he or she is creating*, a perfect union of order and freedom, and as a result, the finished work exhibits the same perfect union.

For solutions, we also need our sixth element, information. We can't solve the problems of quantum mechanics if we don't know physics or write the great American novel if we don't know English or invent an artificial form of photosynthesis without knowing chemistry. The raw data has to be in our brain for our consciousness to connect. As Sir Isaac Newton once said, "If I have been able to see farther than others it was because I stood on the shoulders of giants[97]." His insights into physics and mathematics were built on the information discovered by the likes of Keppler, Galileo, and Copernicus. His consciousness was extremely alert, creative, intelligent, orderly, and free but his consciousness was also full of information.

If Keppler, Galileo, and Copernicus had not lived before him could Newton have seen so far? Solutions are created by an alert, creative, intelligent, orderly, and free consciousness spontaneously combining information in new and original ways but you cannot combine what you do not have. Schools, colleges, and universities are based on the premise of providing individuals with the information they need to create solutions. But it is again important to point out that information itself is inert data. It is in the lively field of awareness that information is organized and combined into a solution which is why alertness is fundamental to information.

But because information takes time to gather— days, weeks, years—as we as individuals and collectively as humankind build our storehouse of knowledge, it is very important that we have the persistence to gather the information AND to stick to the task of solving a specific problem, which is why we need desire, our seventh element for solutions.

Desire has both a mundane and subtle aspect. The mundane aspect is that it prods us to wake up early and stay up late in schools, libraries, and laboratories, gathering information. It is desire that maintains our determination day after day, week after week, year after year to pursue the solution to a problem.

But the deeper and more profound aspect of desire is that *it is desire that impels our consciousness to flow in the direction of greater charm which is the direction of solutions.*

This innocent and yet powerful flow of our consciousness in the direction of greater charm is the subtlest form of desire, and the subtlest form of desire is love. Love is desire. Desire is love. Love is the ultimate attractive force, the ultimate motivator. Due to the tendency of consciousness to flow in the direction of greater charm, we spontaneously become absorbed in subjects we love. If we love chemistry or astronomy, our consciousness spontaneously absorbs itself in those topics.

Love (desire) creates the strongest bond for an individual to pursue information. Love creates the strongest bond for an individual to think about a specific subject. And love creates the strongest bond for consciousness to move within in the direction of greater charm which results in a solution.

We've discussed how the movement of our consciousness can be skipping along the surface, slipping from topic to topic, but once we find a subject we love, our consciousness dives deep, becoming intensely absorbed in that subject. Deep absorption allows our consciousness to sink to levels where our consciousness is more lively and more likely to arrive at solutions. This form of absorption comes from loving a subject.

It is this innocent and effortless absorption in subjects we love which allows our consciousness to maintain orderliness *and* freedom. Think of the absorption that comes when we are engaged in a subject we love. It is strong and deep yet it is totally absent of force. We want to be there, and the more we love the subject, the more deeply "there" we are. Yet no matter how absorbed we are, our consciousness is always free to combine disparate ideas spontaneously, effortlessly, and innocently.

When we don't like a subject, we have to force our consciousness to focus on the subject. And by that force, we prevent our consciousness from flowing in the direction of new concepts, new angles, new notions, and thus fresh, original, and innovative connections are much less likely. How can fresh, original, and innovative connections occur when we are holding our consciousness fixed as if with shackles?

Recall our example of reading a book on a subject we don't like. Even though we might sit in our room or office with the boring chemistry, history, or accounting book in our lap—even though the book is open, even though we are, in good faith, attempting to read the book—our consciousness always drifts away. And we don't even realize the moment when our consciousness drifts away because our consciousness moves in a more charming direction by itself.

On the other hand, when we love a subject, even when we're doing something else, our consciousness *always* has the possibility of returning to the subject we love. Why? Because our consciousness is always ready to move in the direction of greater charm by itself which is why those free mental times when we're shaving or walking in the woods are when solutions on a subject we love often pop up.

Boring tasks dull us. Studying a subject we love keeps us naturally wider awake, and if we want to gather more information about the subject, we can. If we're wider awake, we can bring more creativity and intelligence to the subject. With love, order and freedom reign. Love is the medium, the magic elixir, the cosmic ether for all the elements necessary for the most powerful solutions to occur.

> When you love something, it's a bottomless pool of energy. That's where the energy comes from. But you have to love it sincerely. Not because you're going to make money from it or be famous or get whatever you want to get. When you do it because you love it, then you can find yourself moving up and getting really good at something you wanted to be good at. Will is like not eating dessert or something. It's just forcing yourself. You can't force yourself to be what you have made yourself into. You can love it. Love is endless. Will is finite....Real love is what enables you to accomplish anything. Not discipline. Not work ethic. You gotta love it. If you love it, those other things come in behind. They're the troops behind. Love is the general.[98]
> **Jerry Seinfeld—Comedian**

> The focus is going to come if you are giving it all you got. I think intensity comes from a love of what you're doing.[99]
> **Butch Hobson—Baseball Manager**

> Don't write what you know—what you know may bore you, and thus bore your readers. Write about what interests you—and interests you deeply—and your readers will catch fire at your words.[100]
> **Valerie Sherwood—Author**

Love many things, for therein lies the true strength, and whosoever loves much performs much, and can accomplish much, and what is done in love is done well.[101]

Vincent Van Gogh—Artist

Your work is going to fill a large part of your life, and the only way to be truly satisfied is to do what you believe is great work. And the only way to do great work is to love what you do. If you haven't found it yet, keep looking. Don't settle. As with all matters of the heart, you'll know when you find it.[102]

Steve Jobs—Apple Founder and CEO

Except life does not always present us with problems in fields we love. In school or at work, we are often required to solve problems in areas we don't like. This predicament means that desire can also arise from need. Need is when we don't enjoy the subject we pursue but due to circumstances we are forced to engage in the subject, which doesn't mean we can never solve problems in subjects we don't like. But it does mean solutions will occur less frequently and less profoundly. If a subject bores us and we only think about it out of necessity, the subject remains on the surface of our consciousness. Our consciousness constantly drifts onto other things, and as soon as work or school is over, we completely forget the subject. So if at any time, our consciousness slips into a solution state where all seven elements necessary for solutions are present, while connections on other subjects may occur, connections on the subject we are disinterested in are much less likely.

We can also say not liking a subject reduces the information we need to solve the problem because with subjects we don't like, we don't work as hard to gather information. However, we can solve problems in areas we don't enjoy because of two very important points: 1.) Love is universal and every subject—even a subject we don't like—has some degree of charm, and 2.) every solution by nature is charming whether it is in a field we like or don't like, so, we can expect solutions to occur even when we are dealing with subjects we don't like.

However, it is important to mention that just because we love a subject does not mean that solutions always flow. Even when we love a subject, we do not always have the seven elements necessary for solutions together to the sufficient degree. Even when we love a subject, we can become bored or frustrated or anxious or physically tired or not have sufficient information. But when we love a subject, it does mean we keep at it and thus have the best chance of having together at the right time sufficient levels of the seven qualities for solution.

CHAPTER 12

How the Seven Qualities Work Together to Produce an *"Aha"*—as well as Adrenaline, Alcohol, and Dream Solutions

Now that we know the seven elements necessary for solution, let's demonstrate in a practical way how these elements work together.

For our example, let's say we're in high school and we're studying poetry and are assigned to write a haiku. Since it's a high school assignment, our teacher is not expecting us to be Shakespeare or Matsuo Basho (a Japanese haiku master) and, as our consciousness is a solution system designed to solve problems of lesser and greater degree, we can manage the haiku homework without too much trouble.

Since we're assigned the poem, the element of desire is present. Of course, it's better if we like English and in particular like poetry but, regardless, the task has to be done and, as our teacher is not expecting a masterpiece, our normal mental state should allow for sufficient alertness, creativity, and intelligence. Having attended all our classes, we have the information as to the correct form, and, as we've had a good night's sleep and are not feeling anxious about the assignment, we have the necessary orderliness and freedom. Thus, in this routine, mundane way, we have a state where the seven elements required for solutions are together to the sufficient degree. Obviously the more profound our level of the seven elements, the better the haiku will be. For those who find poetry unpleasant, boring or who have less information (i.e. they have not paid attention in class or have a poor vocabulary), the less good the haiku will be. But, after sitting down at our desk and putt-putting and hem-hawing, making ourself comfortable (i.e., more orderly), we're ready.

Ideas start. Words flow.

Quickly we progress—haikus are short, just three lines—and we're very pleased with ourself. Except, suddenly, seemingly for no reason, we're knocked out of our rhythm. We hit a skip, a blip, a rut, and we're stuck. We've got the first two lines and want to come up with the last line which plays off the first two lines but our mind is blank. No ideas come. Over and over, we try but every attempt sounds stupid. Somewhere in our head, we feel an idea is slinking but it doesn't pop up. We're left grasping, grabbing, groping. We sit at our desk, sweating, struggling, straining. Why doesn't the line or even part of the line appear? When will it flash?

In one way or another, we all encounter blocks like this, big or small. But now the reason is clear. We are simply suffering from a temporary reduction in one or more of the seven elements for solutions. Due to a wave of fatigue, our consciousness may suddenly be cloudy and have lost some of its alertness, creativity, and intelligence. Or maybe we are so surprised our first two lines came quickly, it's brought about a touch of anxiety and we start to force or control, lessening our mental orderliness and freedom. Or if our vocabulary is not good enough, we might lack the information. Maybe we're looking for a few words with the right number of syllables, so that the last line fits the correct form but all our choices have too few or too many syllables. In these situations, a thesaurus might be the answer. But whatever the issue, if we continue straining and struggling, the "*aha*" is not going to appear.

Stuck as we are, here is where the importance of desire (at least, on the level of perseverance) appears. It is desire which keeps us at it, trying to dredge up the right words like repeatedly turning the ignition key of a car, endeavoring to get a balky engine to start. And if we try long enough, hopefully sooner rather than later, we come up with a line that fits.

Keeping at it is always a good thing—desire is one of our seven qualities for solutions—but perseverance should include taking breaks, pausing, resting, walking around, getting a good night's sleep (when possible), and trying again when our consciousness is fresher, calmer, and more alert. Force and effort only delay the answer. Just as it requires the right mechanical conditions to start our car—if we've flooded the engine, we can't keep pumping the gas; we need to wait until the engine drains—solutions require the right mental conditions. Taking a break does not necessarily delay a solution. It may hasten it.

> Don't worry about breaks every 20 minutes ruining your focus on a task. Contrary to what I might have guessed, taking regular breaks from mental tasks actually improves your creativity and productivity. Skipping breaks, on the other hand, leads to stress and fatigue.[103]
>
> **Tom Rath—Author**

But some people persevere in a very forceful way and still come up with an answer. How is this possible?

As the English writer Katherine Mansfield once remarked, "What happens as a rule is if I go on long enough I *break through*."[104] Or Genevieve Grotjan, one of the WWII decoders, is described in the book *Code Girls* as someone who looked for breakthrough insights by sitting "for hours contemplating streams of letters, making notations, creating charts."

However, it is not going on for hours in a forceful way that creates "breakthroughs." What really happens when we stick with a problem without taking a break is that eventually fatigue enters, reducing our level of effort and anxiety. When effort and anxiety are lessened that reduction allows for more freedom and orderliness. At the same time, if the fatigue has not too severely degraded our alertness, creativity, and intelligence, the answer may pop up. It's far easier to take a break, but that is how continuous force when it's applied in these instances works. We get worn out enough so that momentarily, we stop forcing and that free and orderly moment is all the time it takes for the answer to appear. It is the quickness with which the right word or idea materializes that makes it seem like a "breakthrough." But it is not breaking through. It is actually a moment when strain, control, and force lessens.

It's always a matter of balance between the difficulty of the problem, the degree of the seven elements required, and the state of our consciousness. If anxiety and effort are too much, maybe a little fatigue can lessen our apprehension and force and allow for more orderliness and freedom. Or if alertness, creativity, and intelligence are not enough maybe it will only take a pause or in more acute cases a nap or a good night's sleep to restore our ingenuity and imagination. If our information isn't enough, it's back to the library or the thesaurus or the lab. For any solution, there are thousands of variables.

However, in the case of our haiku, as it is just homework, eventually, if we maintain our desire to solve the problem, the answer will appear. The more of the seven qualities, the better the solution; the less, the poorer the solution. Desire plays a big role here—are we willing to wait for a really good solution to naturally pop up or will we settle for practically anything just to get the assignment done? However we feel, whatever we choose, one way or another, the haiku is finished.

Small solutions (or big solutions) mean having together to the proper degree the seven qualities for solution, which, due to the constantly changing nature of our consciousness, helps explain why "*ahas*" are so unpredictable and infrequent.

But what about those times when we need a solution quickly and it has to be a good one? When we can't settle for average? When, perhaps, we're an ad exec and by the end of the day we need to come up with something really catchy for a shampoo or a deodorant commercial.

Sometimes the pressure of a deadline helps result in a solution. Why? Doesn't the stress of those situations create anxiety and disorder?

The stress of time pressure does create anxiety and disorder but it also creates a surge of adrenaline. A surge of adrenaline can be a powerful aid to solutions because adrenaline increases alertness and alertness is the foundation for all the qualities necessary for solutions, particularly creativity and intelligence. But while the enhanced alertness, creativity, and intelligence from adrenaline are a great help for solutions, in these situations it's also extremely important to maintain orderliness and freedom. When we're under the stress of a deadline, panic can engulf us, sweeping everything in its path and our hoped-for solution will be lost. We need increased alertness but also orderliness and freedom.

Athletes and performers often face this situation where before a show or a competition, they feel anxiety—sometimes to the point of vomiting. But pre-performance jitters also cause a surge of adrenaline, and, if the athletes or performers (or advertising execs) can take advantage of the adrenaline and not let the anxiety overwhelm their mental freedom and calmness (orderliness), they can manage their task well. In fact, athletes, performers, or ad execs who attain a good level of alertness *and* calmness don't just manage but excel. This state is so well-known it's been dubbed by athletes as "being in the zone." "Being in the zone" is the athletic equivalent of a solution state. NOTE: some athletes report that they don't get pre-performance jitters. But nonetheless before a game they are going to become excited to some degree, and even a small surge of adrenaline, particularly to a superior athlete who has exceptional qualities of calmness, allows for that athlete to attain the level of clarity, orderliness, and freedom he or she needs to excel.

> The zone is a state of mind which is marked by a sense of calmness. In addition, there is a heightened sense of awareness and focus. Actions seem effortless and there is an increased belief that your dreams or goals can become achievable and real. In addition, there is also a sense of deep enjoyment when the person is in this unique, special and magical state of being.[105]
> **Dr. Jay Granat—Sports Psychologist**

> It's a perfect combination of...violent action taking place in an atmosphere of total tranquility...When it happens, I want to stop the match and grab the microphone and shout, **"That's what it's all about."** Because it is. It's not the big prize I'm going to win at the end of the match, or anything else. **It's just having done something that's totally pure and having experienced the perfect emotion**, and I'm always sad that I

can't communicate that feeling right at the
moment it's happening.[106]
Billie Jean King—Tennis Champion

Being in the zone has become so popular a phrase
that it has seeped into the common lexicon. However, the
prevalence of the phrase does not signify a real understanding
of the qualities that make up the state nor how to make the
state occur or last longer.

> So what does being in the zone during
> athletic competition have to do with me here
> and now well into the "third act" of my life's
> play? I continue to have these moments as a
> businessman, moments that find me. In fact,
> that's the only way they happen, because when
> I actively seek them, they resist and recede. I
> also know that the more fixated I become on
> any end prize—a liquidity event, optimizing
> profit, etc.—the less likely it will happen.[107]
> **Jaffer Ali—CEO pulsetv.com**

But once we know that the "zone" is the athletic equivalent
of a solution state, how the zone occurs becomes clearer. While
we generally think of athleticism as purely physical, sports,
particularly professional sports, requires the same mental
qualities required for solutions: alertness, creativity, intelligence,
orderliness, freedom, information, and desire—however, all
used at the split-second speeds of an athletic contest.

Bill Belichick, considered one of the greatest NFL
football coaches, once said about his strategy to win games:

> You can go all the way back to a few hundred
> years B.C., Sun Tzu, 'The Art of War.' Attack
> weaknesses, utilize strengths and figure out
> what the strengths are on your team. There

> are some things you have to protect. Find
> the weaknesses of your opponent and attack.
> You can't win a war by digging a hole. You
> gotta attack. You have to figure out where
> you want to attack, how you want to attack
> and that changes week to week and game to
> game.[108]

While this quote is from the point of view of a coach on the sidelines, his players have to execute the coach's strategy in real time on the football field and that takes all seven qualities for solutions. The more "in the zone" a football player is, the better the player's ability to fulfill the coach's strategy will be—seeing, reacting, moving, planning, attacking, defending, all with precise coordination between the player's consciousness and body ("violent action taking place in an atmosphere of total tranquility").

Adrenalin, of course, is not going to put every athlete in the zone and not all athletes who are in "the zone" will perform at the same level. Even with a surge in adrenalin, some athletes will still have lesser degrees of calmness or alertness or intelligence than a superior athlete. But if the lesser athletes can increase their usual level of clarity and calmness, they will perform at or near their peak. The key is to allow the pressure of the situation to create the adrenalin surge but not let the surge overwhelm orderliness and freedom.

Since we are now describing in a practical way how solutions occur, we should take the opportunity to explain the seemingly inexplicable fact mentioned in the beginning of this book—that *"ahas"* occasionally take place when an individual is drunk or having a dream, which anyone would think would make for poor conditions for solving problems. However, with our new understanding of how the seven qualities interact, we can explain why an *"aha"* moment can occur in these situations. It is because the missing element for the solution is freedom. We have the requisite alertness, creativity, intelligence, orderliness, information, and desire, but our consciousness is in some way too rigid, inhibited, or controlled to connect already mastered information in original and innovative ways. In this predicament, a dream or a drunken stupor temporarily lowers mental rigidity, giving our consciousness the freedom it needs to make the correct connections. Once sufficient freedom is added to the mental mix, lo and behold, the answer appears.

Of course, when considering solutions, for instance, in drunken states, if we are so inebriated, we can barely think, solutions are not going to occur. Drunkenness is not a formula for "*ahas*". But if mental freedom is the missing element, and we are drunk enough to loosen our mental rigidity, yet not drunk enough to seriously impair our alertness, creativity, intelligence, orderliness, information, and desire (again all related to the difficulty of the problem), solutions are possible. Let's re-emphasize the importance of desire because even when drunk, the desire to solve the problem must be sufficient to bring the problem to our consciousness. Also, we should be very clear that we are not recommending alcohol as a method for solving problems. What we are doing is explaining why these solutions can occur. Getting drunk is far more likely to lead to a hangover than a solution.

Many people believe drugs beside alcohol improve their ability to arrive at solutions. This belief is because some drugs produce an initial sensation of being "high"—a feeling of well-being, along with an alert mental state. However, like caffeine (the mild, socially acceptable drug), this initial "high" never lasts. Before too long negative effects set in and the stronger the drug, the stronger the negative effects. But in the temporary "high," where we can feel very alert and also mentally orderly yet free, a solution is possible.

For a writer or composer or other artist who is desperate to create, any success through the use of drugs increases the temptation to take more drugs regardless of the consequences. Thus, after the "positive" effects of the drug wear off, and only negative effects remain, the individual may, perhaps, feel compelled to continue taking drugs, which in the end produces more negative effects and the goal of increased solutions results in less and less solutions and even tragedy. The list of artists destroyed by drugs is long: F. Scott Fitzgerald, Edgar Allan Poe, Jackson Pollock, Billie Holliday, William Faulkner, Dylan Thomas, Willem de Kooning, Edna St. Vincent Millay, Jimi Hendrix, Janis Joplin, and Jim Morrison to name just a few. Lest this long list tempt us into believing artists need drugs to create, whether or not it destroys them, Tolstoy, Dickens, Chekov, Trollope, Melville, Dickinson, Thoreau, and Austen are just a few of the great artists who did not abuse drugs.

Drugs are not the source of creativity. Consciousness is. If drugs were the source of creativity the world would have many more artists because so many individuals abuse drugs. Drugs cause death and death is the ultimate creative block.

In the case of dream solutions, we should again note that in dreams, consciousness is always to some extent present. There is even a category of dreams called "Lucid Dreaming," where a person is aware that he or she is dreaming and the dreamer is sometimes even capable of consciously manipulating the dream. Lucid dreaming is a state where there is much more awareness than in a usual dream.[109]

It is also common—whether in a lucid dream or not—to dream about what we do. A ballet dancer will dream about the ballet; a painter will dream about painting; a mathematician will dream about math. And *if* we're struggling with a problem and *if* we actually dream about the problem and *if* the dream is coherent and vivid—in other words has more awareness—and *if* freedom is the missing element, then the dream state, where freedom exists to a great extent, may produce a solution. It is a lot of ifs but then dream solutions are not very frequent.

In those instances when we wake up from sleep with a flash of inspiration, whether we awaken in the morning or in the middle of the night—we should once more note the solution does *not* occur in sleep—the solution occurs when we are awake. Yes, it is a wakefulness that occurs very close to sleep but we are still awake.

To explain this experience, think of a night when we have to wake up early, let's say to catch a plane. Dutifully, we set our alarm for 5 a.m. but what happens? During the night, we might wake up 2-3 times before 5 a.m. Why? Because before we go to bed—even though we set the alarm—we are intensely concerned about waking up on time, and because sleep varies in depth, rising and descending like an elevator between light sleep, REM sleep, and deep sleep,[110] during a point where the sleep elevator so-to-speak has risen and sleep is lighter and contains more consciousness, the need to wake up may rouse us into even greater wakefulness (or maybe a noise in the room stirs us). We remember our plane and open one eye and if it's 2 a.m. we groan and go back to sleep, perhaps to self-awaken at 3 or 4 a.m. until, maybe, we awaken at 4:45 a.m. and it's close enough to 5 a.m. to drag ourself out of bed.

But what this familiar experience shows is that if, instead of having an early wake-up impressed on our mind, we have a problem, the rest and relaxation of sleep can restore the seven elements we need for the solution. Thus, in the middle of the night or in the early morning when our sleep elevator is near the surface, our desire to solve the problem can stir us into wakefulness and, like a surfer riding the wave of refreshed alertness, creativity, intelligence, orderliness, and freedom, we can bring our solution to shore.

In these instances, the information is already gathered and learned. The qualities that are usually most lacking are freedom and orderliness but any one or more of the other qualities may be insufficient, and once the refreshment of sleep has restored the lack, we have our solution.

Because the proximity of the solution and sleep we can be fooled into thinking the answer emerges from the depth of sleep but this is a misapprehension. Our unconscious mind is not laboring with the problem during sleep. Sleep revitalizes our consciousness. Sleep restores the elements we need for a solution. Then, when there is a wave of awareness that contains all the qualities necessary to solve the problem, the "*aha*" occurs.

Again, we are not recommending dreams, drunken stupors, and certainly not drugs as methods for solving problems. Drugs are too dangerous and too self-defeating and drunken stupors and dreams are too unpredictable to be practical ways of solving problems. But, at least, we now have a sense of how the seven elements required for a solution interact to produce a solution.

CHAPTER 13

How Consciousness Functions as a Solution System in Relation to the Five Stages of Illumination

We believe the four stages of insight (preparation, incubation, illumination, and verification) developed by Wallas (the fifth stage being the propitious incident stage added later), correctly describe the general behavior leading up to and following solutions. Since we believe Wallas's stages (including the propitious incident) are correct, we need to determine whether our solution system model supports or in any way contradicts these five stages.

Preparation—the first stage—is when we collect the data we need to solve a problem, which certainly agrees with our solution system model. Everyone to some degree is always gathering information through books, TV, the Internet, other people, and our own experiences. Information gathering is one of the required seven elements for solutions and it is undoubtably important. A writer with a 50,000-word vocabulary has a better chance of writing well than a writer with a 20,000 word vocabulary. An artist who has studied many artists is better prepared than an artist who has only studied a few. Scientists in every field need vast amounts of information to solve problems.

However, as we've discussed, the preparation stage is not when problems are solved. Problems are solved during the incubation stage. But, while Wallas's stages of illumination merely state this fact, our solution system model explains it. Solutions never occur during the preparation stage because in the preparation stage the stress and strain of gathering information does not provide the ideal mental conditions for "*aha*" experiences. Thus, a solution will not occur until *all* the information is gathered for a particular solution and our consciousness shifts into a more relaxed mode—the incubation stage.

The preparation stage is not time or location dependent. The preparation stage is defined by gathering information. We can be in a library or an Uber. If the Uber driver mentions some bit of news, it could be the last piece of information we need to solve a problem. Information gathering is not just for when we are in a library or a lab. Information gathering is a task we must do wherever and whenever we are.

But while information gathering is important, solutions require a calmer, freer mental state—the incubation stage. As with the preparation stage, the incubation stage is not location or time dependent. Whether we are at the beach, on a train, or in the office does not matter. What defines the incubation stage is *the state of our consciousness*.

We can be in the preparation stage studying intently in the library and pause and stare out the window and shift into the incubation stage. Then, we can return to our books and switch back to the preparation stage. Since we rarely know when we've gathered all the information necessary for a solution (until the solution appears) and since we naturally alternate between gathering information and mentally resting, for any solution, many incubation and preparation stages most likely occur. There is no set length of time or frequency for either stage. As long as we have the desire to solve a problem, any preparation time could be the one where we've gathered all the information and any period of mental easiness could be the moment when the solution occurs. But while the incubation stage truly distinguishes itself from the preparation stage due to the internal state of our consciousness, external situations do influence our consciousness such as walking in the woods or sitting in the backyard or in the moments before we fall asleep or in the moments immediately after waking up. But inner calmness and alertness can occur anywhere—on a plane, in a car, in a bath, or on an assembly line.

As mentioned, for most of our lives, we go back and forth between the preparation stage and the incubation stage. And if, for instance, we're building a business, we're not working on one problem at a time. We might have ten problems or more to solve, and each one may be in a different state of progress. Since we're intermittently going back and forth between the various stages, we may be having "*ahas*" on some problems, gathering information on others, and verifying other problems.

As for the propitious incident which precedes some "*aha*" moments, our solution system model explains that stage occurring when every element necessary for a solution is present *except* for the missing piece. So, when the final information appears, the solution is instantaneous. Noticing the apple fall was the propitious incident which triggered Newton's consciousness to combine that phenomenon with all the data he already knew about physics and out burst the law of gravity. Similarly, Archimedes perceiving water rise as he entered his bath spurred his consciousness to connect that observation with everything he knew about weighing objects and out sprang Archimedes, shouting, "Eureka!" along with the principle of displacement.

However, as our solution system model emphasizes, the key to Newton's and Archimedes' eurekas is *not* the propitious incident itself. As significant as their observations were, if either man did not have sufficient levels of the other six elements for solution at the time of the propitious incident, illumination would not have resulted. Think of the days Archimedes took a bath or Newton saw apples, coins, or bottles fall yet the propitious incident passed both men by. Why? Because on those days the other elements necessary for a solution were not sufficiently present. However, on the day when both men's consciousnesses were lively with alertness, creativity, intelligence, orderliness, freedom, desire, all of the needed information (except for the missing piece) *and* the propitious incident occurred, that is when we have the whoop, "Aha!" That is when we have the cry, "Eureka!" That is when we have the solution.

Regarding the illumination stage, we've already discussed how our solution system model explains illuminations. Solutions occur because our consciousness has within it the tendency to move in the direction of greater charm, of doing less and accomplishing more, of increased orderliness, and solutions provide the greatest charm, do the least and accomplish the most, and create the most order. So, when left on its own, our consciousness spontaneously flows in the direction of solutions.

That the illumination stage occurs after or (perhaps more accurately) during the incubation stage is because the rest and relaxation of the incubation stage provides our consciousness with the best environment for achieving the higher levels of the seven qualities for solution required.

As for the last of the five stages, verification, it is defined by Wallas as the time spent engaged in the mundane task of confirming the revelation of the illumination stage. On this practical point, our solution system model certainly agrees. Every inspiration, no matter how charming, requires objective verification. When we arrive at a solution, it may be a pleasant idea to us but it is not necessarily the right idea; an *"aha"* experience is the most charming connection we can achieve with our current level of the seven qualities required for solutions. However, our current level may lack an important piece of information or sufficient freedom, creativity, intelligence, or orderliness, and as a result, our "charming" insight may very well be wrong.

Thus, our solution system model both agrees with and establishes a comprehensive and logical framework for understanding Wallas's stages of illumination.

To some, our solution system explanation might seem mechanical, particularly since *"aha"* experiences are so intimate to us and the sensation is so pleasurable. Nonetheless, our consciousness is in some sense mechanical. It moves in the direction of greater charm by itself, and this mechanical movement of consciousness is the key to solutions. However, our own individual will is not left out. We all have different likes and dislikes which determines in what areas we solve problems—be it science, engineering or the arts—and we all have our own levels of desire which determines how much information we gather, how long we stick to a problem, how well we've educated ourselves, and the study and practice we put in.

There are many instances of people with great talent who never use it or do not use their talent to the fullest or waste their talent and lives with drugs or alcohol or antisocial behavior. And we all have our own life experiences which, for a writer or painter determines not only our subject matter but the style and tone of our creations. Many composers can arrive at solutions but only Gershwin is going to compose *Rhapsody in Blue,* only Milton will write *Paradise Lost.* Even in the case of scientists studying objective laws of physics, there is an individuality to what field they work in and how they perform their real or thought experiments. But in every instance of problem solving, it is the state of our consciousness and the seven qualities for solution which determines the profundity of the result. However, as this book will show, we can all as individuals take steps to improve our consciousness and thereby improve our ability to solve problems.

CHAPTER 14

The Solution System and The "Unconscious Mind"

At this point in our discussion, we must confess that our solution system model does conflict with one idea mentioned frequently in the literature on insight. Although our solution system model posits that "*aha*" moments appear instantaneously, many of the famous men and women who describe their insights insist that, despite the swiftness of their "*aha*" moments, solutions are actually "…a manifest sign of long unconscious prior work."[111]

> Having, by a time of very intense concentration, planted the problem in my subconsciousness, it would germinate underground until, suddenly, the solution emerged with blinding clarity, so that it only remained to write down what had appeared as if in a revelation.[112]
>
> **Bertrand Russel**
> **—Philosopher/Mathematician**

> As for the middle theme, it came upon me suddenly, as my music sometimes does. It was at the home of a friend, just after I got back to Gotham. I must do a great deal of what

you might call subconscious composing, and
this is a good instance.[113]

George Gershwin—Composer

I registered the horses as a good subject for
a poem; and, having so registered them,
I consciously thought no more about the
matter. But what I had really done was to
drop my subject into the subconscious,
much as one drops a letter into the mail-box.
Seven months later, the words of the poem
began to come into my head, the poem—to
use private vocabulary—was 'there.'[114]

Amy Lowell—Poet

So much in writing depends on the
superficiality of one's days. One may be
preoccupied with shopping and income tax
returns and chance conversations, but the
stream of the unconscious continues to flow
undisturbed, solving problems, planning
ahead: one sits down sterile and dispirited
at the desk, and suddenly the words come
as though from the air: the situations that
seemed blocked in a hopeless impasse move
forward: the work has been done while one
slept or shopped or talked with friends.[115]

Graham Greene—Author

This unconscious mind is for us like an
unknown being who creates and produces for
us, and finally throws the ripe fruit in our lap.[116]

Wilhelm Wundt—Psychologist

As to why these and other creative individuals believe
their sudden insights are the result of "long unconscious
prior work," we can only speculate. However, one possible

explanation is that it is difficult even for a genius to accept that a complicated problem which has stumped that genius (and perhaps humankind) for many years can be solved—even by them—in an instant. In addition, since experiences of illumination bring the sense that solutions arise "like a gift" from some hidden depth, it is not implausible for them to assume that somewhere in these hidden depths, their unconscious mind worked, occupying itself to solve the problem.

But whatever their reasons, we cannot rely on vague conjectures even from the brilliant. Theorizing as has Bertrand Russell and the others that solutions "germinate" over time might sound credible, but before we accept "periods of long unconscious work" as a real and necessary prelude for the "*aha*" experience, we must establish in more concrete detail what such "unconscious work" would consist of and exactly when our unconscious mind would perform it.

Many of the above quotes begin with the concept of "planting" a problem or the germ of an idea and then having the unconscious mind labor over the problem or idea until the solution occurs. This concept of "planting" does agree with our solution system model. The planting of an idea or problem is nothing other than the creation of a desire and, once that desire is created, it lingers, particularly when it is motivated as in the above instances by a love for the subject.

However, the planting of a problem or an idea is not always going to result in a solution. As a practical matter, let's say we're a poet, we probably plant a lot of ideas for a lot of poems. Some ideas will be stronger than others. Some will require greater degrees of alertness, creativity, intelligence, orderliness, freedom, information, and desire. Some ideas will have more poetic qualities and translate more easily into poems, and each idea requires different levels of information—maybe we want to write a poem about a building we admire in a visit to New York City but we don't know enough about the building or architecture. Or maybe we want to write a poem about a girl we are dating but our feelings for her are still too new for us to define in words and we need to wait until the relationship grows or until the emotion is stronger. These experiences do not need long unconscious labor. They involve growth on the level of information (which includes the maturing of our feelings through life experiences), and a time when alertness, creativity, intelligence, orderliness, freedom, and desire are sufficient to bring the poem into fruition.

Of course, we are not confining this need for time to poetry. Similar types of lacks can delay solutions in every area of life. Long delays between the planting of an idea and its solution are not indications of unconscious work, but rather the constant changing of the state of our consciousness and the infrequency of having all seven elements for solutions together at the same time, and in many instances, a lack of information. Planting an idea and then having the solution occur many months or years later is nothing other than a long preparation stage. We may not consciously be trying to prepare to write a poem about horses, but observations here, the reading of a book there (which might not even be about horses but somehow is relevant because it inspires us with an exciting verb or image or fresh way of expressing an emotion), then, when the seven qualities for solution are naturally present, it might seem as if the poem writes itself. But it is not due to long unconscious labor. It is due to a long preparation stage AND sufficient levels of the seven qualities suddenly being together—and the poem or song or formula is born.

However, since this chapter is devoted to the possibility of unconscious work really being a part of the "*aha*" process, let's ignore the solution system for a moment and examine in more detail what methodologies unconscious work, if it does exist, would consist of and when it would take place.

Clearly, if we are trying to solve a problem, unconscious work does not comprise any of the activity of the preparation stage. Going to libraries, reading, memorizing, carrying out experiments, and just going on about our daily life in all the ways that we gather information are conscious acts—both haphazard and deliberate—and involve interaction with the outside world. Similarly, the propitious incident during which we observe an outside phenomenon such as the rising of water in our bath or the falling of an apple from a tree are conscious experiences. And since they occur at a time when all the other qualities necessary for a solution are present and *immediately* precede an illumination, the propitious incident cannot play a role in *long unconscious* work. Therefore, having eliminated these two stages from consideration, that only leaves some aspect of the incubation stage, a name which Wallas employs because, perhaps, he too believes that it is during this stage that our mind "incubates," performing unconscious labor.

Giving the matter a superficial glance, we might agree.

The rest and relaxation of the incubation stage seems like an ideal time for our unconscious mind to germinate, analyzing a hodge-podge of information and organizing it into a more cohesive structure. As we've discussed, the incubation stage doesn't have to be performed in one continuous stretch. After all, if we are working on a problem over weeks, months, and years, many incubation periods will come and go. But even though these periods might make an ideal time for the mind to work unconsciously, we still have to determine the specific type of problem solving our unconscious mind would use.

Maybe, we might object, since we are talking about unconscious labor how can we ever answer this question with any degree of certainty?

However, mental activity—whether conscious or unconscious—must take place sometime and must, during that time, utilize some type of mental technique. Therefore, if our mind does "germinate" unconsciously, we should be able to discover something about the method of germination and when it takes place.

In our favor, when we investigate, we find that only a limited number of methods for solving problems exist: logic, experimentation, trial-and-error, and intuition. While there may be many variations and combinations of these four approaches, no other techniques for solving problems exist. (Experimentation—whether a thought experiment or a physical experiment—occurs consciously, so we will not discuss it as an aspect of long unconscious labor.)

Since all solutions are orderly, using some form of logic is, well, logical. We can, perhaps, debate the merits of various logical systems but whichever method we choose all logic involves the manipulation of thought through reason. With logical reasoning, we follow ideas out as far as we can. When we get stuck, we rework the ideas. We consider different arguments and examine the ideas from different angles. We juggle concepts back and forth, always trying to find a sequence that make the most sense—does the least and accomplishes the most—is the most orderly, the most charming.

Trial-and-error techniques do not necessarily require logic, however, as we mechanically arrange ideas in different sequences, our goal is to utilize a systematic progression which removes repetition, builds on successes and eliminates failures without any "reasoning" behind our strategy other than trying the most plausible attempts first and keeping to our overall goal of each "trial" being unique until by dint of sheer number we find the correct answer.

From the above descriptions, it should be apparent that logic and trial-and-error are arduous and intricate mental processes. As such, it is difficult to conceive of either going on somewhere inside our head without our being aware of it. The manipulation of thought, whether by rote or by reason, requires a high level of mental activity that would most likely bring our unconscious manipulations to the conscious level.

Intuition is defined by the dictionary as "the power or faculty of knowing things without conscious reasoning; quick and ready insight."[117] However, if we use this definition of intuition (and it as good as any), we see that intuition is also excluded from having any significant role in *long* unconscious labor since intuitions occur quickly, and are essentially what an illumination moment is—when we have the intuition the problem is solved. Long unconscious work is supposed to lead up to the intuition, not be the intuition.

If we protest and say our unconscious mind could perform logical techniques and even trial-and-error techniques in a very effortless, free, and spontaneous way, aren't we then admitting that with this freedom and spontaneity our unconscious mind could perform these tasks quickly and aren't we again approaching the alacrity of the intuitive and thus not needing long unconscious labor? The closer our concept of unconscious work edges to the realm of the spontaneous, the effortless, and the free, the closer we come to the intuitive and the quick, and the more we must concede that "*aha*" experiences do not require hours, days, weeks, and months of unconscious labor.

However, if we're unwilling to abandon intuition as a method of long unconscious labor since it seems so suitable for an "unconscious" mind, what if we consider a series of "small" intuitive "*ahas*" taking place unconsciously over time that lead up to our one big conscious "*aha*." Unfortunately, this theory also runs into problems. The unconscious mind would have to keep each of these small individual insights in some sort of unconscious memory and organize them in some sort of logical way until enough have occurred to create the conscious "*aha*"—again a lot of work for the unconscious mind.

Plus, intuitive solutions, even small ones, are accompanied by a sense of happiness and the physical quality of inner brightness. This inner glow and happy feeling would tend to make an illumination moment conscious, preventing it from playing any role in *unconscious* work.

But what if the unconscious work occurs solely within the physical structure of the brain in an unknown area and in an unknown way?

What if this unexplored part of our brain has a desire for a solution "planted" when we are awake and then this unknown part of the brain works on the problem on its own? But working on a problem means thinking, and whenever we "think," intelligence becomes involved. Thinking about chemistry or physics or music or characters in a play requires a lot of decisions. How do the physical components of the brain make these decisions? How do the physical components of the brain determine what a character in a play says? Or choose what clothes a character wears? Or conceive what the notes of a song should be? Or make-up what the lines of a lyric are? Or what the size of a galaxy is? Or discover what combination of chemicals makes a glue adhere?

Can any part of the brain even be said to hear, see, taste, smell, or feel? The physical structure of our nervous system creates the electrical signals for our brain to interpret but isn't it our consciousness that actually sees the colors, hears the music, tastes the food, smells the flowers, feels the wind? It's like the old question when a tree falls in the forest does it make a sound? Falling trees create sound waves but the sound is only experienced as a sound when our consciousness hears it. Can parts of the brain that have never "heard" a sound create music? Can parts of the brain that have never seen a color create art? Can parts of the brain that have never seen a human being or felt an emotion create a poem? Can parts of the brain solely rely on the chemicals and electric currents created by our senses to organize all the elements of a poem or a symphony or a painting into a coherent and emotionally moving structure?

Let's take music. Music is sounds organized to create beauty and emotion. Our brain like a computer translates electrical signals from our ears into musical sounds. So why couldn't our brain, on its own, compose music solely based on these electrical signals?

The organization of sound into music is based on a sophisticated body of rules, regarding composition. Those rules have been developed over centuries by individuals playing and listening to music, *consciously*. On top of that, Indian, Japanese, and Chinese music, for instance, use different instruments and different rules. It's not instinctive. It's not intuitive. How do the physical components of the brain know these rules? It requires a conscious human being to learn the rules. And, yes, these rules are then recorded in the brain. But even more importantly, it takes a conscious human being to *break* the rules. And every once in a while, we have a genius like a Beethoven, Wagner, Bartok, or Schoenberg who not only breaks the rules but creates new rules. How do chemicals or electric currents decide on their own when to break a rule and when to create new rules and when to obey the old rules and by doing so create immortal masterpieces? It is hard to accept that just the physical components of the brain can accomplish this task and, as a result, compose great symphonies, concertos, and operas (which are also human dramas) without the input of consciousness.

In the 1812 Overture, Tchaikovsky used canons, bells, and French themes to musically represent the victory of Russian forces over Napoleon. A canon is not a musical instrument. Can chemicals and electric currents decide on their own to use canons in a composition? Can chemicals and electric currents decide on their own to incorporate French music into a Russian overture? In Beethoven's *Pastoral Symphony*, he uses musical instruments to sound like birds, brooks, and thunder. Why would chemicals and electric currents decide on their own to do these things and how could they? Have they heard birds? Have they heard thunder or bubbling brooks?

If we want to go through long complex steps where, for instance, a conscious musician learns the rules of music, hears birds, brooks, and thunder and then his or her brain chemicals and electric currents figure out on their own how to musically mimic birds, brooks, and thunder, and then when all is done, decide unconsciously to stick those sounds into a symphony, it's possible. But it requires so many steps and so many wild stretches, twists and turns, and leaps of logic, which goes so strongly against nature's rule of simplicity (doing less to accomplish more). Doesn't it make more sense to accept that human beings consciously hear the sounds and consciously compose the music for other human beings to consciously listen to?

The brain doesn't work without consciousness and consciousness doesn't work without the brain. But it is our consciousness that organizes, our consciousness that desires, our consciousness that plans, our consciousness that combines, our consciousness that knows, our consciousness that hears, tastes, sees, smells, and feels. The physical components of the brain are the tools. Our consciousness is the knower and doer.

We all have the experience of working on something late at night and everything seems in a muddle and then in the morning everything falls into place.

On being very abruptly awakened by an
external noise, a solution long searched for
appeared to me at once without the slightest
instant of reflection on my part...[118]

Jacques Hadamard
—Mathematician

On an occasion I was handed a complicated toy
which was out of order and would not operate.
I examined the mechanism carefully but did
not see how the defect might be corrected. I
resorted to sleep for a solution of the problem.
At daybreak the corrective manipulation
appeared thoroughly understandable and I
promptly set the contraption going.[119]

Cannon—Psychologist

I go on thinking about my problems all the
time, and my brain must continue to think
about them when I go to sleep, because
I wake up sometimes in the middle of the
night with answers to questions that have
been puzzling me.[120]

Albert Szent-Gyorgi—Biochemist

But are the above experiences because our unconscious
mind works on the problem while we're sleeping or is it
because in the morning (or in the middle of the night when
we awaken) our consciousness is now fresher and clearer?
What if in the morning, our consciousness is still in a muddle
(or even more of a muddle)? Do we think the answer will
come? No. Because what solves the problem is not a night of
unconscious labor but a fresher state with all seven elements
for a solution functioning at the necessary levels.

Dream solutions also hint at unconscious labor. We
can consciously "plant" an idea and that "planting" does

occasionally result in a dream solution. But to consider dream solutions as the source of unconscious labor is difficult because, when we talk of *unconscious* labor, we cannot consider *remembered* dreams. We must only consider some form of *unremembered* dreams because it is *unconscious* labor. And for *long* unconscious labor, there must be many unremembered dreams, occurring over many weeks, months, and years and they must all be on the same or a related subject—not a very realistic prospect even for one who has an intense desire to solve a problem.

Recurring dreams do happen, but if "unconscious dreams" are the answer to "unconscious work," then everyone who has had a significant moment of illumination must have had that moment preceded by many unremembered dreams. However, linking many unremembered dreams over many nights all on the same subject is like linking many small moments of intuition. It means our unconscious mind must keep track of the progress: the character development or the plot development or the musical themes or the mathematical algorithms all building on one another—a very complex task for unconscious labor—which makes the concept highly unlikely. The physical components of the brain are good at storing memories but our consciousness is what links the memories into a coherent structure.

We might again object that since our unconscious mind is unconscious and nature is full of surprises, who is to say that a long series of unremembered dreams all contributing to the eventual production of a symphony or poem or play does not take place or that there might not exist some unknown method of unconscious work, dreamlike or otherwise, which produces our solutions. But even so, we must consider that that unconscious method still must occur somewhere and must involve some form of creativity (energy) and intelligence (direction, discrimination).

During deep sleep the most primitive areas of the brain maintain the body's functioning, however, the brain chemistry that supports more complex thinking is low.[121] Higher mental activity, thinking, and creative insights are associated with faster brain wave activity which occur in the waking state, the lightest stages of sleep, and the dream state. All instances of dream solutions occur in remembered dreams—otherwise we wouldn't recognize them as dream solutions. Deep sleep, where unremembered mental activity is most likely to take place, is characterized by the slowest brain waves–the delta waves—the brain waves associated the least with creative thinking. Thus, it seems unlikely that during deep sleep the intricate mental gymnastics required for writing plays, composing symphonies, and solving mathematical equations could go on.

Even if we conjecture some unknown form of thinking that could take place sometime in sleep, the more complex it is, the more active our brain would be, and therefore the more conscious. If we instead imagine this unknown form of thinking to be simple, effortless, and natural, then the more it tends toward the intuitive and the quick. Yet, if despite all of the above arguments, we still cling to the belief in "*long* unconscious work," having eliminated dreaming or sleeping as the times when such unconscious work could occur, we're left with only one other possibility: when we're awake. But that possibility is even harder to accept than long unconscious work taking place during dreaming or sleeping.

When we are aware, we are aware. When we think, we know we are thinking. On a Sunday drive into the country, are we to believe that while we're steering the car, enjoying the scenery, completely unknown to us, another deeper, darker part of our consciousness is occupied, composing blank or rhymed verse or devising intricate mathematical equations or symphonies?

It is common to get "lost in thought" and to have a solution pop up. But being "lost in thought" is not unconscious labor. When we're lost in thought, our consciousness shifts naturally and spontaneously from one thought to another until we slip onto a more charming subject. A subject that we may not even realize we're thinking about, even while we're thinking about it, and because it's charming we go deep into that subject, until some interruption snaps us out and we suddenly realize how intensely absorbed we were. But we're not "lost" or unconscious. We're naturally, effortlessly, and spontaneously absorbed in thinking about a charming subject. This phenomenon of thinking about something and not realizing we're thinking about it, or how long we're thinking about it, or how we got absorbed thinking about it is a common trait of the human thought process.

> Boredom is a very self-conscious emotion by definition. Interest is not. So you can actually be completely absorbed in something and, at certain points in your development, not even realize that you're into it.[122]
> **Angela Duckworth—Psychologist**

Being lost in thought is such an effortless form of thinking these types of experiences often lead to solutions, but again we cannot label them unconscious work.

> How often are creative ideas generated during episodes of mind wandering, and do they differ from those generated while on task? In two studies (N = 98, N = 87), professional writers and physicists reported on their most creative idea of the day, what they were thinking about and doing when it occurred, whether the idea felt like an "*aha*" moment, and the quality of

the idea. Participants reported that one fifth
of their most significant ideas of the day were
formed during spontaneous task-independent
mind wandering—operationalized here as (a)
engaging in an activity other than working
and (b) thinking about something unrelated
to the generated idea. There were no
differences between ratings of the creativity
or importance of ideas that occurred during
mind wandering and those that occurred on
task. However, ideas that occurred during
mind wandering were more likely to be
associated with overcoming an impasse on
a problem and to be experienced as "*aha*"
moments, compared with ideas generated
while on task.[123]
**Shelly Gable, Elizabeth A. Hopper,
Jonathan W. Schooler—Psychologists**

When the above professional writers and physicists were
successfully "on task" they had sufficient levels of alertness,
creativity, intelligence, orderliness, freedom, information,
and desire to produce solutions. They were, so-to-speak, in
the zone. Perhaps, a small zone—a small solution state—but
sufficient for the work at hand. When they hit a rut—became
anxious or tired—or when they reached an important point
in their endeavors that required more of the seven elements
for solutions than they currently had, at that point, they
might have become stuck and tried unsuccessfully to force
their way forward to a solution. But eventually, when they
took a break—stared out the window, walked outside, etc.—
and their consciousnesses in some way re-entered a more
relaxed solution state, it was then they had their "*aha.*" It
was then that the renewed alertness, creativity, intelligence,
freedom, and orderliness became sufficient for a solution and

their desire (love) for the subject brought their consciousness naturally and effortlessly back to the problem and they experienced their "*aha*."

In our difficulties with long unconscious labor, we need to ask, aren't those who believe in long unconscious labor simply burdening their idea of the unconscious mind with the same limitations and restraints they believe their conscious mind toils under? They seem to believe, if the conscious mind strains and struggles for days, weeks, and months over a problem, the unconscious mind must, too. But that conceit not only lacks a clear and practical view of what unconscious work, if it exists, would be, more importantly, it lacks a realistic picture of how effortlessly and quickly our consciousness can function.

Yes, it takes years of study, practice, and experience to gain the necessary information and skill to find a solution but that doesn't mean, for instance, when we finally become a composer that when we're sleeping, quite unbeknown to us, mini-Beethoven brain cells are bent over a desk with quill pens, scribbling and scratching out ideas. But it does mean that on the days when we have sufficient levels of alertness, creativity, intelligence, orderliness, freedom, information, and desire that solutions rise up quickly.

Scientists have found correct answers do not have to be preceded by hours of incorrect answers. Correct answers typically do not even bear any logical relation to incorrect answers. Experiments done at Columbia University on students trying to solve brain teasers selected to simulate the "*aha*" experience demonstrate that failed attempts do not serve as a basis for correct answers:

> Every 10 seconds, students were asked to rate,
> on a scale of one to 10, how close they were
> to the answer. Metcalf found that students

THE SOLUTION SYSTEM

could not predict whether they would solve the problem.

> Those who thought they were "warm" inevitably got it wrong. And those who found the correct answer felt "cold" until they had a breakthrough insight...[124]

Wrong attempts might have value in trial-and-error methods. Wrong attempts shut one more door that no longer has to be opened but they do not bring us any closer to a moment of illumination. A moment of illumination opens a door that by trial-and-error or logic, we most likely never would have opened because it usually comes from a direction far from the routine path we were pursuing which shows that solutions from this new hitherto untried direction occur *quickly*.

The brain and consciousness work at great speeds. Even if we just consider the speed of the physical brain, we find that:

> Brain scientists now tell us there are on the order of 100 billion neurons in our brains, that each one may contact 10,000 others, and that each can send up to 100 messages a second. Modest estimates of the total information processing are upward of 10^{27} bits of data a second.[125]

Our brain and our consciousness do not require long unconscious labor. When conditions are right all the time it takes to come up with a solution is just the flash of an "*aha.*" That is the accurate *description* of illumination and that is the accurate *experience* of illumination.

However, we all spend so little time in the solution state, we've become accustomed to false starts, struggles,

135

and failures and accept them as the norm. But if we look at our own *"aha"* moments and those of others objectively, the evidence shows when conditions are right solutions can and do occur swiftly.

Consider the improvisations of artists like Mozart, Gershwin, Pollock, or Kerouac. While they may have difficulty accepting that they have within themselves the capacity to devise great beauty quickly, if anything, the speed of their improvisations proves their ability to rapidly produce profound solutions.

> I asked him to give me a theme, but as he would not, one of the monks gave me one. I worked upon it till mid-way (the fugue was in G minor) I passed into the major, in playful style but in the same *tempo*; then I returned to the theme, but reversed; and at last I took it into my head to see if I could treat the theme of the fugue in the same joking spirit. I did not have to seek long, but came on what I wanted almost at once, and it worked out as accurately as if a tailor had taken the measurements. The Dean was quite beside himself with delight.[126]
>
> **Wolfgang Amadeus Mozart**
> **—Composer**

Beethoven, Kerouac, Pollock, Gershwin, and Mozart are just a few of the many artists known for their improvisations and spontaneous creations (never forgetting the years of training and study that contributed to the development of their skills). Yet how can long unconscious labor ever be considered a significant factor in performing improvisations when by definition improvisations are created from themes, images, and ideas that are new. It is true that artists occasionally incorporate a few previously prepared ideas into their improvisations but that only means that their improvisations are in part derived from previously prepared ideas, not ideas that are the result of *long unconscious* labor.

The significant factor for any improvisation (or for that matter any work) is always the state of the consciousness of the artist *at the time* the artist is creating. If the artist's consciousness has high degrees of the seven qualities for solution, the improvisation or work is done well and quickly. There are no impediments to block the flow of ideas. If the artist's consciousness has lower degrees of these qualities the improvisation or work is not as well done or completed more slowly. Of course, impediments can always occur. The genius of a Mozart, Beethoven, or Gershwin is that the seven qualities necessary for solutions are present within them for longer periods of time and to a greater degree than for the rest of us which leads to their many "inspired" improvisations and compositions. The subjective experience of sudden illumination is not only possible but far more in agreement with the reality of how the brain and consciousness behave and, as well, conforms to our experience and the reasoning delineated in our solution system model.

In fact, speed is one of the most accurate signs that the creative process is going well. When we create quickly, our consciousness is functioning effortlessly. Of course, we're not talking about sloppiness, or lack of caring. When creating is slow, it is usually due to strain and force. It is hard to connect ideas and what ideas are connected do not have a high degree of charm. Artists, when the full thrust of their creativity is upon them, have no trouble writing, composing, or painting with the swiftness and the urgency of their thoughts. In fact, at such times, the problem usually is keeping up with the blaze of inspiration:

When my work has been quickest done,—
and it has sometimes been done very
quickly—the rapidity has been achieved by
hot pressure, not in the conception, but in the
telling of the story. Instead of writing eight
pages a day, I have written seventeen; instead
of working five days a week, I have worked
seven. I have trebled my usual average, and
have done so in circumstances which have
enabled me to give up all my thoughts for
the time to the book I have been writing.
This has generally been done at some quiet
spot among the mountains,—where there
has been no society, no hunting, no whist,
no ordinary household duties. And I am sure
that the work so done has had in it the best
truth and the highest spirit that I have been
able to produce.[127]

Anthony Trollope—Writer

I cannot really say the book was written. It
was something that took hold of me and
possessed me, and before I was done with
it—that is, before I finally emerged with the
first completed part—it seemed to me that
it had done for me. It was exactly as if this
great black storm cloud I have spoken of had
opened up and, mid flashes of lightening,
was pouring from its depth a torrential
and ungovernable flood. Upon that flood
everything was swept and borne along as by a
great river. And I was borne along with it.[128]

Thomas Wolfe—Writer

The picture is not thought out and determined beforehand, rather while it is being made it follows the mobility of thought.[129]

Pablo Picasso—Painter

As for landscapes, I begin to find that some done more rapidly than ever before are my best. For instance, the harvest and the ricks: it is true that I have to retouch the *whole*, to regularize the composition a bit and make the touch harmonious, but all the essential work was done in a single long sitting, and I touch it as gingerly as possible on coming back to it.[130]

Vincent Van Gogh—Painter

Generally speaking, the germ of a future composition comes suddenly and unexpectedly. If the soil is ready—that is to say, if the disposition for work is there—it takes root with extraordinary force and rapidity, shoots up through the earth, puts forth branches, leaves, and finally blossoms.[131]

Peter Ilich Tchaikovsky—Composer

Ideas came in an uninterrupted stream and the only difficulty I had was to hold them fast. The pieces of apparatus I conceived were to me absolutely real and tangible in every detail, even to the minutest marks and signs of wear… When natural inclination develops into a passionate desire, one advances towards his goal in seven league boots. In less than two months I evolved virtually all the types of motors and modifications of the system which are now identified with my name.[132]

Nikola Tesla—Inventor

One day I was waiting in my car while my wife was out on an errand. I had had for some months some basic information from the laboratory which was incompatible with everything which, up until then, I knew about the photosynthetic process. I was waiting, sitting at the wheel, most likely parked in the red zone, when the recognition of the missing compound occurred. It occurred just like that—quite suddenly—and suddenly also, in a matter of seconds, the cyclic character of the path of carbon became apparent to me, not in the detail which ultimately was elucidated, but the original recognition of phosphoglyceric acid, and how it got there, and how the acceptor might be regenerated, all occurred in a matter of 30 seconds…[133]

Melvin Calvin—Scientist

As these quotes show, when inspirations do, in fact, come, they almost always arrive in a rush. Speed in creation is a sign the seven qualities for solution are functioning as they should. Speed in creation is a sign of a solution state that can continue for minutes, hours, days, and weeks.

One other important point: even though someone like Gershwin was a musical genius that does not mean he was a genius in every field. Using our solution system model, we can see that when it came to music, Gershwin had all seven elements for solutions together often but he did not necessarily have the same level of those qualities in physics or engineering or chemistry. Certainly, he lacked the information and probably also lacked the desire. Maybe physics and chemistry bored him. Music was his element. He felt comfortable (i.e., loved the piano) which allowed him to feel free and orderly when playing. In a high school chemistry lab, perhaps, he felt bored or anxious (i.e., he hated it). But with music he could use his highest level of the seven qualities for solution, while in the chemistry lab, high levels of those qualities, perhaps, deserted him.

When we say "music was his element," what we are really talking about is "talent." "Talent" is also considered a mysterious quality in that some people seem to be born with an innate skill at performing a specific task, often, but not necessarily, in the arts such as Mozart or Mendelsohn who exhibited great musical skill at very early ages. Such talents are hard to explain but our solution system model does shed some insight into these "miracles."

Talent and/or ability is a combination of the seven elements required for solutions, predominating in a specific area. For example, musical talent means we have a high degree of alertness, creativity, intelligence, orderliness, freedom, information (we learn quickly and retain more of what we learn), and desire in the area of music. When we have talent in an area, we feel easy and relaxed in that area. This relaxation (orderliness and freedom) means when we study and play an instrument (or paint or write or work as a mechanic or an engineer or whatever), we are not stressed or anxious. It usually means we love the subject (have a strong desire for that field), so we love to study it, work in it, gain information about it. We probably also have physical attributes that make functioning in that area easier such as if we're a musician, we may have particularly sharp hearing, the coordination between our fingers and brain when we play is excellent; we probably have an exceptional musical memory in that if we hear something we can remember very precisely the order of the notes that we hear; and if we're a singer, we may have qualities in our throat that give a pleasing tone to our voice. An athlete often needs a certain height, weight, eyesight, and level of coordination.

A supportive environment is also important to nurture latent skills. We've mentioned, Mozart's father was a musician and music teacher, Gershwin's parents were not musicians but they supported his musical ambitions. When Gershwin showed a love and skill for the piano, his parents supported his ability with lessons by very well-recognized piano teachers.

> He (George) studied piano with the noted instructor Charles Hambitzer, who introduced his young student to the works of the great classical composers. Hambitzer was so impressed with Gershwin's potential that he refused payment for the lessons; as he wrote in a letter to his sister, "I have a new pupil who will make his mark if anybody will. The boy is a genius."[134]

Gershwin already was showing great skill at the piano. He loved it and had the physical skills (great hand and eye coordination and good hearing) and the mental skills (he could read music easily and learn and remember the rules of musical composition) but he also needed the proper instruction for his genius to blossom, which he was able to receive from his teachers and his own personal musical pursuits.

Other people with insufficient talent may lack some physical or mental skills or access to the required information or due to some aspect of their upbringing—a bad teacher or an upsetting experience—may find a task, to some degree, anxiety producing or may find practicing too boring and not work hard enough at developing their skills.

Thus, talent could be said to be a preponderance of alertness, creativity, intelligence, orderliness, freedom, information, and desire in a specific area supported by a physiology that enhances these qualities and an environment that allows for that talent to grow. However, lesser talent can be overcome. Love is a great motivator and if someone loves art or music or football, he or she can still gain great skill in the field. Countless examples exist of individuals who have less physical or mental gifts but still achieve great things.

> We are told that talent creates its own opportunities. But it sometimes seems that intense desire creates not only its own opportunities but its own talents.[135]
>
> **Eric Hoffer**
> **—Writer and Philosopher**

However, from all available data, what we see is that human beings can and indeed do reach solutions quickly. Speed is not a barrier to solutions but in fact a sign that a task is going well. Long unconscious labor is not necessary for "*aha*" experiences. What is needed are the seven elements for solutions.

CHAPTER 15

The Unconscious Mind

In the last chapter, we hoped to show that the "*aha*" experience is not the result of long unconscious labor.

Does this mean that an unconscious mind doesn't exist?

No.

Ideas originate within the field of our consciousness and we have described this field at its most fundamental level as a field of pure awareness. When an idea begins, it is a faint impulse rising from this field. Imagine a bubble rising from the depth of the ocean. In the depth of the ocean, it begins small. At such a small size, it will never be visible to someone on the surface. In the same way, because of its faintness, an idea is as if invisible from the surface thinking value of our mind. When an idea begins, it is so faint it is unrecognizable as a thought or feeling.

> Such intuitions give the appearance of miraculous flashes, or short-circuits of reasoning. In fact they may be likened to an immersed chain, of which only the beginning and the end are visible above the surface of consciousness. The diver vanishes at one end of the chain and comes up at the other end, guided by invisible links.[136]
>
> **Arthur Koestler—Author**

The beginning is the desire for a solution. The ending is the "*aha*". The invisible phase is the connection which occurs at or near the field of pure consciousness and is what we can term "subconscious." But by calling it subconscious we do not mean anything Freudian or Jungian or any other "ian". It is subconscious simply because it occurs so deep and is so faint, our surface level of consciousness cannot perceive it. This experience of the birth of an idea from the deepest levels of consciousness to the surface level is why solutions are described as the result of long unconscious labor or as a gift or as coming from a dark, mysterious source. It seems like a contradiction—darkness or a mysterious source in a field of awareness—but the phenomenon exists and understanding this phenomenon explains the seemingly baffling experience we've referred to and quoted accounts of throughout this book. The rising upward of a solution is because in reality every "*aha*" has four phases of existence. These four phases should not be confused with Wallas's stages of intuition. These four phases deal with the moment of the *aha*, the flash itself.

Even though an "*aha*" is almost instantaneous and *not the result of long unconscious work*, we can describe its four phases as: 1.) the unmanifest phase where the solution exists purely as potential within the flat, unbounded field of pure consciousness; 2.) the connective phase where the solution is formed by the combination of two or more bits of data at the subtlest levels of thought due to the nature of consciousness to move in the direction of greater charm by itself; 3.) the growth phase where the solution develops, gaining more distinct form; and 4.) the fully developed phase where the solution is grown sufficiently to be perceived, which is our "*aha.*"

All solutions follow this path. Not all solutions will be correct. Solutions always need to be verified, but whether the solution is correct or incorrect, the process is the same. If one or more of the seven qualities for a solution is not strong enough or is missing (insufficient information is a major culprit here), the solution may very well be wrong. And remember the vast majority of solutions are every day solutions, not profound answers to the deepest questions of life. Most solutions are how to sell a new computer product or how to end a history paper or how to fit a large tub into a small bathroom.

But whatever the solution, the reason it appears as if from some mysterious depth is because *the first three phases of solutions occur in that part of our consciousness we can call our subconscious because it is as if hidden from our conscious thinking level.* Obviously, in terms of time, the gap is very short, nonetheless it is a gap—and it is this gap, which produces the sense of the bursting upward of ideas from a mysterious source. However, the rising upward of ideas does not originate from some dark, mysterious source. It is the deepest levels of our own consciousness.

When we think of complex ideas beginning as faint impulses, it may seem impossible that a complex equation or a plot for a play could emerge from such a faint beginning. But it is like a seed that a giant oak tree springs from. The seed, although small, contains all the elements of the tree. When an idea begins it is like that seed. All aspects of the idea are in their most basic, compressed form. The idea has not yet developed, it has not yet sprouted its roots and branches and leaves and thus the idea connects easily and quickly in the deepest levels of our consciousness.

As the idea rises and becomes clearer, the details take shape; the individual characteristics become more apparent. This development is why ideas have to be verified. The idea has to fit reality. The words have to be written on the page or the equation has to be proved or the bridge has to be built. But whether right or wrong, due to the gap between the faintest birth of the idea and our ability to perceive it, the subjective sense of our idea emerging from a mysterious source has turned into the belief in an "unconscious creative mind," perhaps, related to but different and separate from our conscious mind. However, the reality is that from the field of pure consciousness to our conscious surface level is one field of awareness. The source of our ideas, our so-called "subconscious mind," only seems separate and distinct because it is as if veiled by the inability of our conscious mind to perceive it.

Perhaps some might think that this admission of a subconscious mind contradicts the previous chapter where we disputed the existence of long unconscious labor but the operative word was meant to be *"long." Long unconscious labor.* It was about a subconscious mind working during sleep for days and weeks and years on a specific problem, or working while we're awake for weeks and months and years about some problem completely different from what the surface level of our mind is engaged with, or the physical components of the brain working for days, months, and years, performing creative mental labor completely unbeknownst to our conscious mind.

But as we explained in Chapter 10, our consciousness is a solution system and it works naturally, effortlessly, and *quickly.* Yes, our consciousness connects ideas in its own depths where movement is freer, easier, and more spontaneous and then the idea bursts upward to the surface level of our mind as our *"aha."* But this solution process occurs swiftly and it occurs during a pause on the surface level of our mind. Perhaps a very quick pause but a pause nonetheless. We're not thinking of two things at once. The surface level of our consciousness is not thinking of doing the laundry while the depth of our consciousness is working on mathematical equations. The surface level of our consciousness and the depth of our consciousness are not two separate consciousnesses. They are one whole that works together. So, it is possible to be thinking of doing the laundry but then there is a pause, and again it can be a very quick pause such as while we are looking out the window or getting out the detergent or sorting our socks, and it is during this pause that our consciousness has the freedom to move in the direction of greater charm by itself i.e., the problem we've been wondering about and, if all the other qualities necessary for a solution are also present, the "aha" occurs.

However, the question is: if pure consciousness is a field of awareness, and if solutions develop within this field, why are we not aware of our ideas, no matter how faint, from their birth? How, in a field of awareness, can a gap in experience exist? How in a field of awareness can a solution as if develop in darkness and burst upward? How can our conscious thinking level ever be unaware of its own source?

If the basis of our consciousness is what we call pure consciousness (the screen)—an unbounded field of calmness, stillness, alertness, and orderliness—how can our consciousness ever descend into a field of confusion, chaos, and darkness?

This question has one simple answer: stress.

CHAPTER 16

Stress as the Source of the Problem System

It may seem simplistic to say that the cause of the gap in our consciousness is stress, but if we look at the situation carefully, we see stress is indeed the culprit. But what do we really mean by "stress?"

Since a more exact explanation is necessary to understand how stress affects our consciousness, we will define the word as any mental, physical, or emotional experience powerful enough on some level to damage our physiology. As Hans Selye, M.D., the great modern researcher on stress, explains: "In its medical sense, *stress is essentially the rate of wear and tear in the body.*"[137]

Stubbing our toe or hitting our thumb with a hammer are obvious examples of physical stress. Mental and emotional stress is a little less obvious but nonetheless clear. If mentally or emotionally we are upset, a whole range of physiological reactions take place, and these reactions are capable of producing damage that is just as real as any injury. If we're about to give a speech, we get "butterflies in our stomach." If we see a bear in our path, "our heart pounds." If we spot a parking ticket on our car, our "blood boils."

These are common expressions we use to explain the physical reactions we experience when faced with stressful situations. However, while these expressions use colorful, dramatic words, their meaning in terms of the "wear and tear" that occurs to our body is real. Stressful experiences, particularly when severe and/or repeated, result in physical damage to our body. Even positive emotional experiences can create harm. We can win 400 million dollars in the lottery and become so excited we have a heart attack. But what is important to note is that what these examples demonstrate is that the source of most stressful experiences is not physical but emotional and that our consciousness and our emotions do not function in isolation. Whenever our consciousness experiences any kind of thought or emotion, our body immediately produces a reflection of that thought or emotion.

Again Hans Selye:

> An enormous amount of work has been done by physicians in connection with problems of psychosomatic medicine. In essence, this specialty deals with the bodily (somatic) changes that a mental (psychic) attitude can produce. An ulcer of the stomach or a rise in blood pressure caused by emotional upsets are examples in point.[138]

The more powerful our thoughts or emotions, the more powerful the physiological reflection. Therefore, no matter what the source of our stress, the end result is that on some level our body is affected. However slightly or severely, our muscles, organs, glands, blood and/or bones are damaged and this damage lasts. It might take days, weeks, or months to go away or it might never go away. The lasting quality of this damage helps explain why, even though the nature of consciousness is to move in the direction of greater happiness, our mind is often a whirlwind.

When our consciousness experiences some form of emotional or physical stress the damage from that stress is transferred to our body. However, what is important about this connection is that it works both ways. That is the blessing and the curse of connections. Our consciousness influences our body but our body also influences our consciousness. If A is connected to B, and A influences B, what is to prevent B from influencing A? They are both connected so the possibility of influence is mutual.

> When stress affects the brain, with its many nerve connections, the rest of the body feels the impact as well. So it stands to reason that if your body feels better, so does your mind.[139]
> **Hans Selye—Endocrinolgist**

> It is clear that the activity of the mind influences the activity of the nervous system, this in turn causes the release of neurotransmitters and neuropeptides, along with a number of specific physiological changes which then may act back on the nervous system and influence the state of the mind.[140]
> **R. Keith Wallace—Physiologist**

Fatigue is a very common stress, and while it has many causes, it has a very obvious physical component. Not getting enough sleep causes a reduction in our mental clarity.

> Dr. Charles Pollak, head of the sleep-disorder center at Cornell University's New York Hospital in Westchester County (declares), "[Sleepiness] doesn't make it difficult to walk, see or hear. But people who don't get enough sleep can't think, they can't make appropriate judgements, they can't maintain long attention spans."[141]

According to a study conducted in Canada, on the day after people move their clocks ahead an hour (and thus lose an hour of sleep), traffic accidents increased by 7 percent.[142]

When you get too little sleep, you build up a sleep debt, much like continued spending builds up a monetary debt. Each day with insufficient sleep increases this debt. When this sleep debt becomes large, you have problems...[143]

But as serious as sleep deprivation is, how many of us get the sleep we need?

At 7 a.m. or 6 or maybe even 5, the blare of the alarm breaks the night, and another workday dawns. As an arm gropes to stop the noise and the whole body rebels against the harsh call of the morning, the thought is almost always the same: *I have to get more sleep.* That night, after 17 or 18 hours of fighting traffic, facing deadlines and racing the clock, the weary soul collapses into bed once again for an all-too-brief respite. And just before the slide into slumber, the nagging thought returns: *I have to get more sleep....*[144]

This sleep debt when continued over years contributes greatly to our buildup of stress because the weaker and foggier we are during the day, the more susceptible we are to stress. We get angrier quicker or have more accidents or perform less well in our studies and our office work, which leads to more stress.

And fatigue from lack of sleep is just one example of physical stress influencing our consciousness. If our body is hurt, our consciousness feels pain. If our body is massaged, our consciousness feels pleasure. If our body needs food, our consciousness feels hunger. *And if our body is bent, knotted, and twisted from the build-up of stress, our body is going to reflect that stress back into our consciousness in the form of restless, worried, negative, and disorderly thoughts.*

Let's examine how this build-up of stress affects us in more detail. Let's say we have a difficult client at work. We call this client every day, and because each call is stressful, each time we speak our hand grips the phone tighter. In other words, the emotional anxiety is directly transferred into the muscles of our hand, arms, and shoulders. Perhaps, it is also distributed into other areas of our body. Maybe our heart beat increases, our lungs breathe faster, and our adrenal glands pump out increased levels of adrenaline. In other words, A is influencing B—our consciousness is affecting our body. However, at home in the evening, when we no longer have any reason or desire to think about the office and it's in our best interest to forget, worried, restless, and negative thoughts still haunt us. While we're eating supper or trying to go to sleep, thoughts of that difficult customer swirl.

Why? Because the physical disorder from the stress is imprinted in our body and our body reflects that disorder back into our consciousness. Even though we're at home occupied with other pursuits, we still can't get those unpleasant thoughts out of our head. As long as that stress endures in our body, it will continue to influence our consciousness. Now, B is influencing A. The stress in our body is influencing our consciousness.

Consider for a moment all of the physical habits and mannerisms stress induces: cigarette smoking, fingernail biting, gum chewing, hair twisting, knee shaking, etc. These nervous habits and mannerisms do not appear only when we are at work or in some other stressful situation. They persist with us over time because the stress in our body persists with us over time. As a result, we must ask, if the level of stress in our body is powerful enough to cause physical changes in our behavior such as cigarette smoking, nail biting, gum chewing, knee shaking, and hair twirling, how much easier is it for that same stress to influence our consciousness, which is much more sensitive and malleable?

As long as a specific stress or group of stresses persists in our body, the disorder from that stress influences our consciousness. It must because our consciousness and our body are a two-way street. *Our consciousness influences our body and our body influences our consciousness.* And since our consciousness is where we reside, to the degree that our body contains stress, we, the ego, the I, the experiencer lives in a tense, restless, anxious world. Thus, the accumulation of stress over the years causes what we can call a *general physiological stress level.*

In other words, on a normal day even when nothing is bothering us, we are not totally calm. From events in the past, we still have an accumulation of stress. All those difficult customers, traffic jams, arguments, disappointments, and missed sleep leave their mark and that includes positive experiences as well. We've mentioned how winning the lottery can give someone a heart attack. And it's not just extremes. Both good and bad experiences—big and small—damage our body and feedback into our consciousness.

Another illustration. Let's say we are moving out of state because of a better job. If we have difficulty selling our house and our anxiety level rises, a typical refrain is to promise ourself over and over as soon as we sell our house, we'll be happy and never worry again. And part of that promise is true. The pressure of selling the house is making us worry.

But part of that promise is not true because when we do sell the house *all* our worries don't go away. We still worry because of our general physiological stress level. Selling the house may cause a momentary feeling of elation, and our anxiety may lessen but the calm never lasts. Due to our general physiological stress level worries flood back. Before too long, we find ourself worrying about buying our new house. Then, when the new house is bought, we worry about our kids getting along in their new school or exorbitant property taxes or politics or the economy or maybe some challenging aspect of our new job.

If, at any moment, there aren't any big problems, we worry about small problems. Even when there aren't any new problems, we dredge up old problems. Sometimes, we even seem to make up stuff to worry about because our general physiological stress level keeps our consciousness on edge. As our circumstances change, the subject matter of our worries may change. Our stress level might fluctuate from day-to-day and major incidents—both for good and bad—cause swings in our stress level, but over the long term, our general physiological stress level always influences our consciousness, *which is why we rarely have all seven qualities necessary for solving problems together to the proper degree.* How can our consciousness maintain a sufficient level of these qualities when stress continually roils our consciousness?

Thus, it is the influence of stress on our consciousness that explains why, even though our consciousness is a solution system, answers often elude us. The seven qualities for solution never function at their peak if our consciousness is disturbed by the influence of stress. Stress inhibits our consciousness from maintaining a solution state.

Stress is also responsible for that gap in our awareness. At the end of Chapter 15, we wondered how in a field of awareness could we ever have an interruption in our ability to perceive? Now, we understand why. The gap in our awareness between the birth of an idea and our recognition of it is due to the disturbing influence of stress. Stress not only causes restless, worried, and negative thoughts but clouds our consciousness's ability to perceive at or near the field of pure consciousness.

In the physical world, when we want to observe an object that is hard to see, we enhance our vision with telescopes or microscopes. Yet, no matter how powerful these devices are, the faintest blemish in the lens, the slightest haze in the atmosphere, the feeblest tremor of the earth decreases the instrument's ability to observe, measure, and record.

In the same way, the smallest worry or fear, the least anxiety or excitement, the merest dullness or fatigue muddies our consciousness's ability to discern our thoughts at the subtlest levels. When our consciousness is turbulent, hazy, or dull, subtle distinctions are impossible. A windstorm is not the time to look for something on the ground.

As a human instrument, to operate successfully at the deepest levels of our consciousness, we need the optimum conditions. We need to develop the ability to function on the level of "inner silence," and by that term we do not mean simply an absence of noise like turning the TV off. By inner silence we mean the absence of "internal noise." True inner silence is the absence of all stress-driven physiological activity and the absence of all stress-driven mental activity. True inner silence indicates maximum orderliness in our consciousness and maximum orderliness in our body. But the problem is most of us do not have sufficient inner silence which is why our consciousness has this gap.

The internal "noise" from stress continually clouds our consciousness and we are unable to perceive at the subtlest levels of thought. Yet this lack is never recognized as a loss because the inner noise has always been there. We take the influence of stress as the norm because even on days when we feel wide awake, our consciousness is not completely clear. Our gap is still there.

Our gap is there from birth.

Just as some of us are born smarter or duller, more coordinated or less coordinated, calmer or more anxious, we are all born with bigger or smaller gaps. Why? Because even in the womb, we're susceptible to stress. Everything a mother experiences from what she eats to what TV show she watches to what she feels affects her physiology which in turn affects her baby's physiology. We don't generally think of fetuses as having stress but they do.

When a baby is growing in the womb, it shares the mother's body and all the chemical and physical reactions going on in the mother's body are going to affect the baby's body. We know smoking, alcohol, and other drugs negatively affect a baby's body. A baby can be born with a mother's addiction and diseases. But while these are extreme situations, everything going on in a mother's body affects the fetus. And just like a mother has a general physiological stress level, the baby will also develop a general physiological stress level, even before the baby is born.

> "When the mother is stressed, several biological changes occur, including elevation of stress hormones and increased likelihood of intrauterine infection," Dr. Wadhwa says. "The fetus builds itself permanently to deal with this kind of high-stress environment, and once it's born may be at greater risk for a whole bunch of stress-related pathologies."[145]

> Most recently, some studies are suggesting that stress in the womb can affect a baby's temperament and neurobehavioral

development. Infants whose mothers experienced high levels of stress while pregnant, particularly in the first trimester, show signs of more depression and irritability. In the womb, they also are slower to "habituate" or tune out repeated stimuli—a skill that, in infants, is an important predictor of IQ.[146]

"Who you are and what you're like when you're pregnant will affect who that baby is," says Janet DiPietro, a developmental psychologist at Johns Hopkins University. "Women's psychological functioning during pregnancy—their anxiety level, stress, personality—ultimately affects the temperament of their babies. It has to…the baby is awash in all the chemicals produced by the mom."[147]

Certainly, immediately, after we're born, our experiences affect us. It doesn't take much to make a baby cry and it doesn't take much to make a baby laugh. Newborn babies are very susceptible to stress.

From birth, babies are learning about safety and trust. Every time a parent or caregiver meets an infant's needs, he or she builds bonds and learns that someone cares—and that stress is limited and manageable. The earliest needs in life include not only feeding and clothing a baby but also responding to a child by providing attention, affection, contact, and comfort to him or her. When an infant's basic needs aren't met regularly, he or she releases higher levels of stress hormones, including cortisol. Stressful experiences in early infancy and increased cortisol levels can have a permanent effect on the brain, impacting attention, memory, emotions and stress management throughout life.[148]

Ages 1–3: From separation anxiety when leaving parents or caregivers to social anxiety in new situations with other children, from learning to use the potty to changes in the family such as a new sibling, toddlers are often stressed by new experiences. Toddlers who experience or witness conflict, violence or neglect at home; are exposed to traumatic events or scary TV or movies; or have a very stressed or depressed parent are especially vulnerable to high stress levels. Stressed-out toddlers may have delays with speech, cry, have frequent tantrums, or be very withdrawn. They may also have problems with concentrating, sleep, digestion, or getting along with or trusting others.[149]

The input of stress begins in the womb and does not stop, which is why we all have gaps in our consciousness. Our general physiological stress level and our daily stresses hinder solutions, but it doesn't prevent them. We are conscious and consciousness is a solution system. However, both forms of stress explain why solutions seem to burst upward out of darkness onto the surface of our consciousness. Hopefully, now the quote from Koestler makes more sense.

Such intuitions give the appearance of miraculous flashes, or short-circuits of reasoning. In fact, they may be likened to an immersed chain, of which only the beginning

and the end are visible above the surface of
consciousness. The diver vanishes at one end
of the chain and comes up at the other end,
guided by invisible links.[150]

We are working on a problem (planting a desire), gathering information in various ways—studying, experiencing, researching—and whenever the "noisy" influence of stress quiets (when we pause, look out the window, talk to others, etc.), that is when the seven qualities necessary for solutions can possibly unite and the seeming mental miracle of "*aha*," eureka, and solution moments burst upward. But even when our consciousness seems quiet, it is like a pond with a layer of silt on the bottom. Our consciousness is not totally clear. Due to our general physiological stress level, we still have a muddy layer in the depth of our consciousness, which is why we have the experience of the "*aha*" as if bursting upward out of darkness. The gap in our awareness is not a barrier; it is a fog. Our consciousness is one undifferentiated whole from the field of pure awareness to the surface level and solutions can pass through it. Solutions pop up through our gap all the time—big and small. The more turmoil and fog, the less frequent the solutions and the lower the quality of the solutions. The less turmoil, the less fog, the more solutions, the higher the quality of the solutions. It is always a matter of degree.

But does this swirling, dark haze, this gap, mean that we are all forever fated to function below our human potential? Must we see our brief glimmers of solutions quickly extinguished by the cloudy noise of stress which is what makes these fleeting experiences seem so extraordinary and the quest for them so quixotic? Must we eke out our life as what we can call a problem system? A system burdened with a "stressed" body; and a "stressed" consciousness; a system where we try to solve problems with severely limited resources—all while we have a consciousness that, by its nature, is a solution system?

Fortunately, the answer is no.

Even though the corporeal structure of our body makes us inevitably subject to stress, even though our body is forced to endure the "thousand natural shocks the flesh is heir to," we can find a way to improve. Nature has provided its own cure.

Just as our consciousness is a solution system, our body is a solution system. Even though our body is a physical structure, indeed because of it, physiological processes exist that permit us to reduce stress. Just as the natural principles that govern our consciousness allow it to move in the direction of greater charm and reach solutions, natural principles exist within our body which allow it to reduce stress, and thereby reduce the gap in our awareness and function better as a solution system.

CHAPTER 17

The Main Principle that Governs the Body, Allowing it to Reduce Stress

Due to consciousness's abstractness, most people consider it a mysterious realm.

This mystery, however, does not extend to the body. The body is completely and obviously physical. The body is flesh, bone, blood, mucous, and spit. It is eyes, ears, feet, hair, and toes. Every inch of it inside and out can be measured, poked, and explored. So the knowledge that the body operates according to physical laws should not be foreign to us. We're all aware of the precise, mechanical, orderly nature of our body. Every aspect of our cells, nerves, muscles, teeth, organs, DNA, and RNA all work according to precise, mechanical principals that science can discover and know.

But is there anywhere in this precise, orderly, mechanical system we can find a method (or methods) which allows us to eliminate stress? In the vast storehouse of medical knowledge is there any law (or laws) which indicate how our body can heal itself?

As we hinted in the previous chapter, there is. A fundamental principle exists and, moreover, this principle is not very obscure, complicated, or esoteric. The search for this principle does not require a great length of time or great depth of research. We're all acquainted with the principle whether we're a doctor, a scientist or a layman. *The principle is very simple—it's rest. Our body heals itself through rest. Our body reorders itself through rest.*

We've discussed how life's joys and sorrows, ups and downs, gains and losses, frustrations and satisfactions, failures and successes bend, knot, and twist our body. Every day, all day long, experience shows stress builds. By 10, 11, or 12 p.m., our body is so worn out, so fatigued, so disorderly, our only option is to go to bed and shut down our entire system. However, after seven, eight or nine hours of this temporary shutdown we call sleep, an amazing thing happens. We wake up refreshed. Our body regains order. We are once more energetic and ready to act. Thus, during the night something happens which allows our body to renew itself. Some physiological process takes place that allows our body to eliminate some of the damage from stress and what that something is, is REST. Simple, natural rest. Through rest, our body eliminates stress. Through rest, our body heals itself. Through rest, our body reorders itself. Through rest, our body regains its normal functioning.

It is an obvious experience to all of us. Whenever we are tired or ill, even if no one else tells us, our body bids us rest. If we get a cold, we stay in bed so that our body cures the disease through rest. If we strain a muscle, we avoid using that muscle so that our body heals it through rest. If we break our leg, the doctor puts it in a cast to mend it through rest. Every part of our body naturally heals itself through rest.

> By sleeping or otherwise reducing bodily activity as much as possible, we allow the body to mobilize its resources for the activity of healing. We must sleep periodically or we become ill, and the deep rest of sleep is so crucial to the proper functioning of the mind and body that it's part of every doctor's

prescription for virtually every disorder. Sleep is so important to the prevention and mitigation of stress-related disorders because, physiologically, the body orders and de-excites itself, the opposite of what happens during the fight-or-flight response.[151]

Healing is a process of becoming more orderly and rest is what allows this process to take place. *Thus, the simple, natural principle, which allows our body to eliminate stress is rest.* The body's tendency to heal itself through rest allows us to eliminate stress and improve our physical orderliness. What greater solution system can there be than an organism that heals itself! Of course, some injuries and/or diseases are so severe they require the assistance of medicine and doctors but rest still plays the major role in healing. Any medicine or treatment a doctor administers merely enhances the body's natural immune system. According to Sir Hans Krebs, Nobel prize-winner in physiology, "The physician and the patient can do no more than assist nature, by providing the very best conditions for [the] body to defend and heal itself."[152] And the most conducive condition for healing is rest.

Of course, sometimes, rest and medicine are not enough. Sometimes the disorder from whatever the cause is too strong and the body is overcome by the stress. But that does not refute the basic principle that the body has within it the ability to heal itself.

Rest has two qualities: duration and depth. How long a period of rest does our body require and how deep a level of rest must our body reach? The more serious the damage, the deeper the level of rest and the longer we need to maintain it. But, unfortunately, as our own experience tells us, while the rest we get through sleep (our main source of rest) is long enough and deep enough to eliminate much of our superficial wear and tear from the day's activities, and even heal many injuries and diseases, it is not long enough or deep enough to eliminate more severe stresses.

The reality is, if a good night's sleep were able to eliminate *all* of our stresses, no one would suffer from chronic health problems such as ulcers, bad backs, hypertension, high blood pressure, and heart disease, which result most often from accumulated stress. Every night, we would rid ourself of the day's stresses and wake up in the morning ready to operate at maximum efficiency. But this is not the case. A good night's sleep does not eliminate all of our stresses. It does not eliminate all of our worries and anxieties. It does not reduce our gap. A good night's sleep restores us to approximately what we think of as our "normal" level of functioning, which means our general stress level is still there. The rest we get from a good night's sleep is good enough to eliminate or reduce many of the day's stresses but is not sufficient to reduce or eliminate our deeper stress and thus does not affect our general stress level. A good night's sleep does not increase the clarity of our consciousness beyond what we customarily consider "wide awake;" while a bad night's sleep leaves us with far less than our normal functioning and renders us vulnerable to gaining more stress.

In such a plight where sleep loss is endemic to society and where even on the nights when we get a good night's sleep it's not physiologically profound enough to release our deepest stresses, is there anything we can do to improve as a solution system? Or are we fated to live life as a problem system: a system stuck in a cycle of increasing stress—the stress in our consciousness creates stress in our body and the stress in our body creates more stress in our consciousness and on and on and on. Because of the mutuality of influence, the cycle constantly feeds back on itself.

For example, when we fall asleep, our consciousness gets duller, duller, and duller until we reach the blackness of sleep. But if we are highly stressed, falling asleep is difficult. When we lie in bed at night, our thoughts keep swirling. We toss and turn and it takes hours to fall asleep, which means we don't get enough sleep, and that fatigue results in more stress. Or if we manage to fall asleep, we may wake up in the middle of the night with our thoughts racing, which prevents us from falling back to sleep, resulting in more stress. In this way, sleep fails us and instead of reducing stress, we gather more stress, which is just one instance of a problem system feeding back on itself—getting worse rather than better.

But the mutuality of influence between our consciousness and our body can also work in a positive manner. It's supposed to work in a positive manner. Just as we've established that disorder in our consciousness creates disorder in our body and disorder in our body creates more disorder in our consciousness, order (calmness) in our consciousness creates order (rest) in our body and order in our body creates more order in our consciousness. Which means our sleep can get rid of more stress, and depending on the depth and length of our rest, perhaps even reduce our gap, which is the hallmark of a solution system, increasing in clarity not fogginess.

NOTE: By emphasizing rest in this chapter, we do not mean to advocate avoiding activity. Activity is good. Activity is life. We live in the movie. We should enjoy it. But one of the best ways to enjoy the movie is to improve as a solution system, and one of the best ways to improve as a solution system is to increase our ability to achieve deep rest. There's an old saying, "The best preparation for an exam is a good night's sleep," and this saying does not have merit only for exams. A good night's sleep helps all our endeavors.

But as sleep does not eliminate all of our stresses and sometimes it's difficult to even fall asleep, where can we find the deep rest we need to eliminate our deepest stresses?

CHAPTER 18

Techniques that Help Create Rest

Over the thousands of years of life on earth, various techniques have been developed and promulgated as ways to reduce stress and increase the orderliness in our consciousness. Some of these techniques are more effective than others—some directly increase rest; some increase rest in a more indirect manner. But they all aim to allow us to increase our functioning as a solution system.

Nutrition is an area that is often promoted as a way to improve health and reduce stress. At first glance, nutrition seems far from a process related to increasing rest. However, nutrition is related to our metabolism. Digestion requires a lot of energy. Proper nutrition puts less strain on our digestive system, provides our mind and body with the proper nutrients, and allows our body to function in a more efficient and orderly way. Good nutrition even helps us sleep better.

> Ana Krieger, MD, MPH, Medical Director of the Center for Sleep Medicine at New York-Presbyterian and Weill Cornell Medicine, tells NBC News BETTER, "Eating an overall healthy and nutrient-rich diet affects our brain health and activity—and in turn, our sleep," she explains. "Eating healthy and allowing the body to absorb proper nutrients provides the brain with the chemical

environment that it needs to produce the neurotransmitters that it needs to maintain adequate sleep," Krieger says. The nutrients we get from food serve as the building blocks for other minerals and proteins that are needed to create the amino acids that are involved in sleep.[153]

Certainly, we know an unhealthy diet causes many health problems such as obesity, high blood pressure, high cholesterol, heart disease, and diabetes.

Today more than 95% of all chronic disease is caused by food choice, toxic food ingredients, nutritional deficiencies, and lack of physical exercise.[154]
Mike Adams—Author

Illnesses are severe shocks to our system and a diet unhealthy enough to cause disease diminishes our ability to function as a solution system. Illnesses do not prevent solutions, but they seriously impair our functioning. However, while eating well helps us maintain what is considered a "healthy" and "normal" physiology i.e., the right weight and no obvious physical diseases, a good diet will not reduce the stress from a divorce or an abusive boss. If all day long someone yells at us, eating more fruits and vegetables is not going to bring major relief. A healthy diet is good but it's not that good. A healthy diet aids our body in reducing some of the toxins produced by being the brunt of constant yelling but it's not going to eliminate all of them or even most of them. A healthy diet is not a sufficient fix for our bigger stresses. A healthy diet helps maintain our "normal" mental state, a mental state in which we sometimes reach solutions but often do not.

As thousands and thousands of books exist on nutrition, it is not necessary to repeat their advice. However, in general we can say, eat more fresh fruits and vegetables, eat less red meat, consume fewer sugar rich foods like cakes, pies, cupcakes, and pastries, eat less processed and salty foods, and drink less alcohol.[155]

Exercise is another technique many people adopt to eliminate stress. Like nutrition, exercise at first glance seems to have little relation to gaining rest. Exercise raises our metabolism and seems the opposite of rest, but exercise increases the orderliness of our body which over the long term contributes to less wear and tear on our physiology. When we first start to exercise, we might huff and puff, but if we exercise regularly, eventually, we will perform the same physical tasks more effortlessly with only moderate increases to our breath rate and heart rate, i.e., doing less and accomplishing more. This physiological refinement means that over the course of our life, our metabolic rate will function more efficiently, even including those periods of exercise when our breath rate is higher.

Exercise has a positive effect on a wide range of stress-related problems.

> When the PA (physical activity) and stress relationship is explored, it has typically been within the perspective of improving mental health outcomes via exercise. As suggested earlier, those who exercise have lesser rates of depression, negative affectivity, and anxiety. Indeed, PA (physical activity) and exercise have been demonstrated to promote positive changes in one's mental health and ability to cope with stressful encounters. Moreover, exercise interventions appear to improve one's depression status.[156]

And like nutrition, exercise can improve our sleep.

> "We have solid evidence that exercise does, in fact, help you fall asleep more quickly and improves sleep quality," says Charlene Gamaldo, M.D., medical director of Johns Hopkins Center for Sleep at Howard County General Hospital... Moderate aerobic exercise increases the amount of slow wave sleep you get. Slow wave sleep refers to deep sleep, where the brain and body have a chance to rejuvenate. Exercise can also help to stabilize your mood and decompress the mind, "a cognitive process that is important for naturally transitioning to sleep," says Gamaldo....People who engage in at least 30 minutes of moderate aerobic exercise may see a difference in sleep quality that same night. "It's generally not going to take months or years to see a benefit," says Gamaldo. "And patients don't need to feel like they have to train for the Boston Marathon to become a better sleeper."[157]

But while exercise is helpful, if exercise were really the solution to the elimination of stress and the reduction in the gap in our consciousness, then marathon and cross-country runners, soccer players, hockey players, and basketball players would all be solution systems. They would all live long, happy lives and be the recipients of "*aha*" solutions almost every time they had a problem, which isn't the case. Exercise is helpful to maintaining a normal state of health but, like eating well, it is not a path to eliminating our gap and profoundly increasing our functioning as a solution system.

Like nutrition, there are thousands of exercise books and styles of exercise but in general we can say moderate exercise is better for the physiology. Strenuous exercise not only physically exhausts but may damage our hips, feet, knees, arms, shoulders, back, and most importantly—our heart.

What is a strenuous workout for one person might be a moderate workout for another person. It depends on our weight, height, lifestyle, etc. A carpenter will engage in more physical exercise during the day than someone who works at a computer. Thus, the carpenter might be more physically fit and capable of more vigorous exercise.

What type of exercise is best? Exercise that we can do regularly, exercise that fits most easily into our lifestyle— walking, jogging, biking, etc., and exercise we love. Do not overdo it, particularly at the beginning when enthusiasm is highest, and the body is weakest. Watch out for two important signs that we are exercising too intensely:

1.) Feeling dizzy or weak for an extended period of time after exercising.
2.) A racing heart long after exercise[158]

The above doesn't mean we shouldn't play tennis or basketball or whatever, but it does mean if we are a thirty-five or forty-year-old businessman or woman, we need to use common sense, and gradually build up our stamina. No pain, no gain is not the formula for successful exercise.

Yoga is very popular these days as a means of releasing stress. Yoga can be considered the subtlest form of exercise because unlike Western exercise it does not significantly raise the metabolic rate. It is thousands of years old and is designed to lower stress and produce good health by stretching and bending rather than running and jumping.

The concept behind yoga is that it releases stress by the manipulation of the muscles and joints through various postures. Each posture is designed to release stress in a particular area of the body and simultaneously create a state of calm. For example, padhastasana, or touching the toes, is designed to improve digestion, help internal organs like the liver and kidneys, and calm the mind.

Unfortunately, the body is not very flexible and is much less powerful than our consciousness. Many people find yoga postures difficult and do not have the patience or perseverance to perform them diligently. It is true we do not have to perfect a posture to benefit from it. Someone can easily touch their toes; someone else can only get halfway or a quarter way. But with yoga, just the attempt releases stress. The question is: how much stress? If we're working to pay the rent or the mortgage or our child's college tuition, is the relief provided by touching our toes going to help? Certainly, a little, but in order to significantly increase the benefits, we have to spend more and more time practicing the yoga, which is rarely feasible, and even then it is probably not going to relieve the stress caused by our overdue mortgage payment. And if we spend too much time doing our yoga, we won't have sufficient time to earn the money to pay the mortgage.

Nonetheless, yoga is helpful. It's best learned from a qualified instructor and practiced regularly. Twenty to thirty minutes of daily yoga exercises will make us feel better, improve our flexibility, and relieve stress but it will not significantly reduce our gap or turn us into a fully functioning solution system.

Meditation is another ancient technique designed to purify our body and our consciousness. Because it is a mental practice, it has the potential to be very effective. As we've said, our consciousness is more flexible and more powerful than our body. Meditation, which was once thought of as something out of the main stream, is now popular. But there are many types of meditation.

Some people think of meditation as what we may call contemplation—quietly thinking about things—usually things of a more serious nature such as the meaning of life or God or the nature of reality. These types of meditations are on the level of the intellect but, since philosophical thinking is a relatively calm pursuit, these meditations can produce a mild degree of rest. However, since the level of rest achieved is minimal, the effect on reducing stress is also minimal. Other types of meditation are those that endeavor to achieve inner peace (silence in the mind and body) through some form of concentration and control. These types of meditation are more in line with what we want—a deep level of inner peace—but trying to achieve a deep level of inner peace through concentration and control is not effective.

Concentration and control techniques usually involve focusing on an object: a picture, a pleasant thought, a memory, the breath, or a part of the body (often relaxing different body parts in an orderly sequence from the feet up). But these types of techniques are not easy to practice and generally do not produce deep rest. In a meditation involving focusing on a thought, we can analyze the thought as in a contemplative meditation, trying to discern its truth or purpose or we can focus on the thought simply as a way to incorporate its *meaning* into our current state of mind. For instance, if we concentrate on peace or joy or love, it's because we want, at least temporarily, to embody those qualities. But, unfortunately, the thought of peace is never peace. The thought of joy is never joy. The thought of love is never love.

We've spent a lot of time discussing pure consciousness, which *is* at the deepest level of our mind, and the surface value of consciousness (the movie) which involves our thoughts and senses. If we meditate by focusing on a phrase, meaning, memory, image, breath, or body part, we are locking our attention onto an object. Words, memories, images, the breath, and certainly body parts are objects and all objects are aspects of the movie. Thus, concentration and control keep our consciousness at or near the surface and, as a result, our mind will not reach the screen (pure consciousness), where real peace, joy, and love reside.

Moreover, telling ourselves to be peaceful when we are highly stressed does nothing to relieve our stress. It's like the *Seinfeld* TV show where George Costanza's father, Frank, repeats "Serenity Now!" when he's angry and upset. However, repeating "Serenity Now" (or thinking it) is never going to make a highly stressed person serene. In addition, focusing is a technique we employ when our consciousness is bored and wants to shift away from the object, which is why we're trying to focus on it. Thus, by definition, any technique which requires concentration means that the task itself is boring and inevitably condemns our consciousness to the surface. Only a technique that employs charm as its reward allows us to become absorbed and dive deep.

Some forms of meditation try to achieve silence directly and quickly—not by concentrating on a thought or memory, etc., but merely by blanking out our mind. The theory is, if we can stop our thoughts, we will then exist in the screen and our body will correspondingly experience deep rest. But blanking out our thoughts is not easy. Continually being on guard to beat down thoughts is yet another form of activity. No matter how hard we try, thoughts jostle, shove, and push their way in. Even if we have some success and manage to clear out most of our thoughts, the attempt is never completely successful because trying not to think in itself requires a thought. We have to be constantly vigilant that we're not supposed to think and that vigilance, however subtle, is a thought. As long as we know that we're not supposed to think, our consciousness has to remain aware that we're not supposed to think, which means on some level we're always thinking.

Mentally the exercise might go like this—*Don't think. Don't think. Don't think. Oooops. Telling myself not to think is a thought. Don't think of anything, not even not to think. But if I don't tell myself not to think, I'll think. Oooops. Still thinking. Try harder. Mind, be quiet. Oooops still thinking. Why is it so hard not to think. Aaaaaaaargh. Mentally screaming seems to prevent thoughts but isn't a scream a thought? Ooops. Thinking again. I wonder what time it is. How long have I been doing this? Ooooops. Still thinking. Hmmmmmm.*

Is there no hope?

Is meditation always fated to be a struggle? A promise of peace but more a mirage than a reality?

Throughout history, the experience of pure consciousness is not very common and is usually mentioned, if at all, as a valuable but extremely difficult state to attain. Everyone seems trapped in the movie unable to reach their own silent depths.

What is wrong?

CHAPTER 19

How the 12ᵗʰ Principle of Consciousness Helps Increase Our Functioning as a Solution System

If we haven't made it clear yet, let's make it clear now. The key to the experience of inner silence is not concentration, control, contemplation, exercise, diet, or stretching and bending. The key is the experience of pure consciousness. By regularly reaching pure consciousness, our mind gains greater inner silence and, as a reflection of that mental silence, our body gains the profound rest it needs to release its deeper stresses and improve as a solution system.

But how do we reach pure consciousness?

In Chapter 6, we explained eleven principles of consciousness, but we left out one important principle—a twelfth principle. As our ability to reach pure consciousness is based on this principle, we need to mention it now. Very simply, our twelfth principle states—*pure consciousness is charming.*

How do we arrive at this principle?

In previous chapters, we've discussed that pure consciousness is orderly and that orderliness is doing less and accomplishing more. We've also shown that doing less and accomplishing more is subjectively experienced as charm, therefore, we can say pure consciousness is charming. Moreover, pure consciousness is not just charming. It's extremely charming. Why? Because merely by virtue of its existence, pure consciousness allows us to experience everything—seeing, hearing, feeling, tasting, smelling, and acting. Talk about doing less and accomplishing more!

But how is the charm of pure consciousness relevant to our reaching it?

Since our tenth principle states that consciousness moves in the direction of greater charm and our eleventh principle states that consciousness moves in the direction of greater charm *by itself,* our consciousness should naturally be able to move within and reach this charming field of pure consciousness *on its own.*

But it doesn't.

When we think of reaching inner silence, people most often think of that task as being very difficult, if not impossible. Yet, despite its difficulty, we all still yearn for the experience. We all want inner peace and, at some point, have probably tried to reach some level of inner silence, usually by attempting techniques we've already dismissed as not being very helpful such as concentrating on some positive thought or image or trying to blank out our mind. But rarely, if ever, do these exercises allow us to experience pure consciousness and, in fact, actually cause more frustration than contentment.

Does this mean the principles of consciousness presented in this book are incorrect? If pure consciousness is charming and our consciousness moves in the direction of charm *by itself,* why do we not reach pure consciousness automatically whenever we want?

This question is easily answered.

Our consciousness works according to all twelve principles we have described but, as a practical matter, when we are young, the first skills we are taught are not techniques for reaching pure consciousness, they are for surviving and succeeding in the movie. After all, we live in the movie.

177

We have to eat, find shelter, wear clothes, and avoid being eaten by animals and run over by trucks, so the main tool we employ is language.

Language is designed for navigating through the labyrinth of life. Thinking, speaking, and performing complex tasks are made possible by language. All of civilization is based on language. Language permits us to master all our other skills—math, science, physics, art, business, sports, etc. Language allows us to express all the ideas and desires continually bubbling up in our heart, mind, and throat. But as important as language is, language actually hinders our ability to reach pure consciousness because with language, we incessantly shift from thought to thought to thought, keeping on the surface of consciousness. Paradoxically, even when we use language to think about silence, our consciousness is not silent. It is thinking about silence and thinking is the opposite of silence. Thinking is an activity. And, once we learn a language, we are as if trapped in its noisy, busy world.

Words confine our consciousness by the walls of their meaning. As long as we are engaged in thinking or speaking, we are stuck in the movie of our life, a movie only occasionally broken by the slumber of sleep and by the even stranger movie of dreams. Words do not provide any escape.

Even though our consciousness always moves in the direction of greater charm, when it flows using language, it flows based on the meaning of the words. If we like history, we read history books. If we like science, we work in a lab. If we like TV shows and movies, we watch TV shows and movies. Yes, we experience moments of "sinking within" when we become absorbed in the *objects* we're enjoying. But pure consciousness is much deeper. It is beyond objects, which is why to reach pure consciousness we need to learn a new technique, a technique for transcending. A technique that does not keep us trapped on the surface. A technique that follows the natural tendency of consciousness to move in the direction of greater charm, *diving deeper and deeper and deeper within*. And, surprisingly, such a technique is not very complex or obscure. The technique is actually very easy to learn. But to understand how such a technique works, we have to understand a little more about language.

Language is based on sound. Cats meow. Dogs bark. Cows moo. But because of the sophistication of our physiology—our lips, tongues, teeth, and vocal chords— human beings are capable of making a wide variety of specific sounds. A language utilizes these specific sounds and puts them into an order we call the alphabet. Every language has an alphabet. The look of the letters may differ, their order may differ, but the sounds are similar because they are the sounds that humans can make. A, B, C, D, E, etc.

In kindergarten and first grade, we spend a lot of time learning the alphabet and how to correctly pronounce all of the letters. Then, we learn how the letters make words and, most importantly, we learn the meaning of these words. Of course, by kindergarten and first grade, we already have an extensive vocabulary but, as we progress through school, we learn more and more words and more and more meanings and explore language's intricacies of grammar and spelling. But always the most important aspect of language is meaning.

Every language has words that define objects, concepts, actions, and emotions. This combination of the sound of the words and the meaning of the words is what permits us to communicate and think in very complex ways. But in the sometimes beautiful, sometimes terrible merry-go-round that language keeps us on, the problem is we can't get off. Language has no shut off switch. When we learn a language, the meaning of the words always keeps our thoughts going from object to object to object, which is why we all occasionally yearn for inner silence.

However, one technique of meditation, the Transcendental Meditation technique®, allows us to escape the merry-go-round. That is why it is called transcendental. Transcending is what the technique is about. Transcending is what the technique is designed for. Its purpose is to transcend the movie and reach the screen (pure consciousness).

The Transcendental Meditation technique achieves this result because it is different than meaning-based language. In this technique, an individual sits comfortably in a chair with the eyes closed (having the eyes closed begins the disengagement with outward objects). Then, the individual uses a meaningless word or sound called a mantra, which the individual thinks. (The word "mantra" comes from Sanskrit, an ancient Indo-European language.) Because the mantra is meaningless, we are not propelled from thought to thought in any specific direction based on the meaning of the word. When we are given the mantra, it leaves our consciousness awake and alert, yet as if suspended, undirected, free. When there is no meaning to keep our mind on the surface, the nature of consciousness follows its tendency which is to move in the direction of greater charm. And since pure consciousness is very charming, our consciousness innocently and effortlessly moves within to ever deeper, more charming levels of our consciousness until we reach the most charming level: pure consciousness.

We do not prod, or push. Our consciousness becomes more and more absorbed in this inner direction *by itself.* Just as when we dive into a swimming pool, we let gravity do the work—so when we practice TM®, we let the nature of consciousness to move in the direction of greater charm do the work. Concentrating and controlling only impedes our progress. The TM technique is natural and effortless. NOTE: We do not spend the entire meditation in pure consciousness. We might only spend a second or two. But we are always "diving" within, experiencing deeper levels of inner awareness.

This book is not intended to teach TM. To reach pure consciousness, we need two important items—the mantra (which is selected for the individual by a TM teacher) and the way to use the mantra, which must be effortless. The instruction is a delicate process and any confusion along the way leads to force and control which makes the technique ineffective.

Correct meditation cannot be "picked up" from a book. One of the most common questions from people learning to meditate is, "Am I doing it right?" A book cannot tell if someone is "doing it right." A book cannot hear experiences and answer questions. To meditate correctly and know that we are meditating correctly so that we are not always wondering, doubting, and questioning, we need a teacher.

The term "expansion of consciousness" is another phrase tossed about these days without much clarity or comprehension. But enlivening the deepest parts of our consciousness and lessening the darkness of our gap is what the expansion of consciousness truly means. Through correct meditation, we have less of a sense of hidden depths or a mysterious source because we function closer to the source. As the static of noise from stress abates, we truly begin to "see."

> If you have a golf-ball-sized consciousness, when you read a book, you'll have a golf-ball-sized understanding; when you look out a window, a golf-ball-sized awareness; when you wake up in the morning, a golf-ball-sized wakefulness; and as you go about your day, a golf-ball-sized inner happiness.
>
> But if you can expand that consciousness, make it grow, then when you read that book, you'll have more understanding; when you

look out, more awareness; when you wake up, more wakefulness; and as you go about your day, more inner happiness.[159]

David Lynch—Filmmaker

To find the best ideas you have to go deep within yourself. To do this I practice Transcendental Meditation twice a day, every day, and by doing so I believe it keeps the ideas coming."

Oliva Locher—Photographer

When you're thinking about creativity, it comes from a source—an inner source. When you're [TM] meditating, you're bringing your consciousness to that centered source of creativity and intelligence. In my opinion, it's the best way to tap into creativity.

Tosin Abasi—Guitar Player/Musician

Scientific studies support these experiences. For example, an EEG study conducted on college students at American University shows:

[TM] produces a unique state of "restful alertness," as seen in the markedly higher alpha power in the frontal cortex and lower beta and gamma waves in the same frontal areas during TM practice.

[TM] creates greater alpha coherence between the left and right hemispheres of the brain suggesting the brain is working as a whole.[160]

And, of course, just as our consciousness is highly alert and orderly, our body is in a deep state of rest, which allows for the release of stress. Other studies done on the Transcendental Meditation technique reveal that as an individual's mind settles down into the field of pure consciousness, signs of deep rest occur throughout the body:

> (a) deep rest as indicated by a marked and significant decrease in oxygen consumption and carbon dioxide elimination.
> (b) significant decreases in respiration rate, minute ventilation, and heart rate.
> (c) deep relaxation as indicated by a significant and sharp increase in skin resistance.
> (d) normal maintenance of critical physiological functions as indicated by stable arterial levels of partial pressure of oxygen and carbon dioxide, pH and blood pressure.
> (e) significant decrease in arterial blood lactate[161]

This deeply restful yet alert experience is the foundation of how we grow as a solution system. The silence of pure consciousness produces the silence of deep rest and the silence of deep rest produces deeper silence in our consciousness. These two experiences continually enhance each other in a cycle of a solution system improving itself. As stress is something we've accumulated all our lives, we need to practice meditation regularly to allow it to work most profoundly. However, scientific evidence verifies that even over the short term, reaching pure consciousness results in significant improvement:

> …In the area of nonverbal fluid intelligence, Tjoa (1975) showed that nonverbal, analytic, and logical reasoning increased significantly in TM participants over 12 and 16-month periods… Abrams (1972) found better performance on

both short-term and long-term recall in those practicing the TM technique. MacCullum (1974) found increased creativity, as measured by the Torrance Test of Creative Thinking (verbal); in another study Travis (1979) found that subjects practicing the TM technique for five months showed a significant improvement in figural creativity tasks, in comparison with a control group... Miskamin (1973) found increased spontaneous organization of newly learned material into taxonomic groups. Pagano and Frumkin (1977) found that TM meditators showed improvement in tonal memory, indicating an improvement in right hemispherical functioning. Finally, in several studies, the academic performance of TM program participants has been shown to improve, as measured by increasing grade point average in college students...[162]

Many people ask, what does pure consciousness feel like? Pure consciousness feels like ourself. It feels like the innermost core of ourself because it *is* ourself. And even though the subjective experience is hard to describe, we know the experience of pure consciousness is real because it can be measured.

Farrow and Hebert (1982), as part of their extensive analysis of periods of respiratory suspension during the TM program... (found that) periods of respiratory suspension were highly correlated with the subjective experience of pure consciousness... Inspection of the EEG showed bursts of beta activity immediately after the end of the respiratory suspension periods. Delta band power was usually low and stable before and during these episodes. Averaged signal tracing showed that theta band power peaked sharply at the onset of breath suspension periods and decreased sharply at the end… EEG coherence in the alpha and beta bands was high before and during the first half of the respiratory suspension period, decreased gradually during the second half, and then decreased abruptly at the end of the period.

In a more recent study (Badawi et al., 1984) the preliminary results of Farrow and Hebert were replicated in a much larger group involving more than 100 subjects and including several additional meditating and nonmeditating control groups.

From these EEG studies as well as the other physiological studies on breath suspension during the TM technique, it appears there are distinct physiological correlates associated with the experience of pure consciousness… These studies have noted specific periods of low metabolic rate, respiratory suspension, and high intra and interhemispheric EEG coherence in alpha and theta frequencies, especially in the frontal and central areas of the brain…[163]

Thus, in the specialized language of science we have a neurophysiological description of pure consciousness. The words are technical but the chemical analysis of an orange would sound equally abstruse. Yet the fruit is real, the taste is sweet, and to take a bite is easy.

Do not deny yourself the pleasure or the benefit.

CHAPTER 20

Other Practical Steps for Growing as a Solution System

Our consciousness is not an adequate solution system or a good solution system. It is a *perfect solution system*.

There are no problems our consciousness can conceive that it can't solve. Our consciousness is not only a perfect solution system because it solves problems, it is a perfect solution system because it has within it the ability to improve.

Reaching pure consciousness through meditation is the most practical way to function better as a solution system. If we do TM regularly, the benefits will be significant, cumulative, and are scientifically verifiable. But as we've discovered, although in a much smaller way, it's also helpful to eat well, sleep well, and exercise (yoga and/or regular exercise).

Something as simple as **when** we work on a problem can also improve our ability to solve problems.

It is a commonly observed phenomenon some seekers of solutions work best in the morning; others find their work is best done at night. This difference is because, while the state of our consciousness always fluctuates, specific periods occur in any 24-hour cycle when our consciousness is clearer or duller. Obviously, our daily activity, and in particular our sleep and eating habits, influences the state of our consciousness. But leaving aside these variations, the state of our consciousness fluctuates due to our natural body rhythms. Scientists have discovered what are called "circadian rhythms," which effect things like our sleep patterns, our eating habits, and even our body temperature[164]. These same rhythms also effect the clarity and lack of clarity of our consciousness. Traditional schedules—going to bed near sunset and rising near sunrise—fit in best with our circadian rhythms, but modern technology and our modern lifestyle (city lights, TVs, bars, etc.) has made listening to our bodies and following this natural routine difficult. We're left adrift as to how best to schedule our eating, sleeping, and working.

> The average adult today sleeps 7 to 7.5 hours each night. In 1900 (before Edison invented the modern light bulb), the average person slept nine hours each night. This means that today's population sleep 1.5 to 2 hours less than people did early in the century.[165]

Today, work hours are scheduled every which way. People can start work at almost any time and end at any time, all while there are specific times, due to our circadian rhythms (which still go on even if we ignore them), where our alertness is naturally brighter and better able to solve problems. For example, most people have a strong wave of wakefulness sometime in the morning. Our alertness might kick in at 7, 8, 9, or 10 a.m., depending on when we go to sleep, how well we've slept, etc. This morning period of maximum wakefulness is an ideal time to solve problems. Between 1 a.m. and 3 a.m. is another period of mental liveliness and a possible time for solving problems. Often, we might feel sleepy around 10 or 11 p.m. but if we push past that fatigue, we get a second wind and start feeling more alert. This second wind is due to our late-night period of mental liveliness.

Interestingly, even though modern technology and the loss of traditional lifestyles puts most of us out of touch with our circadian rhythms, creative people usually stumble upon either the morning or the late-night period for creativity. However, working late at night and not getting enough sleep negatively impacts our health. Still, many people who suffer from anxiety over their creative process end up procrastinating and doing their creative work late at night. They might say they write at night to enjoy the silence and the solitude, and those two qualities are indeed a positive part of late-night labors, but the reality is due to anxiety about their work, procrastination has turned into a habit. It's always better to stick to traditional schedules. Going to bed around sunset is not realistic for modern life but a bed time of 10 p.m. and rising at 6, 7 or 8 a.m., and doing creative work in the morning is best.

Morning Creators

I make each day feel special by starting out creating. When I was younger, I wrote late in the day—and I wrote comparatively little. But for the last ten years I've gotten up and gone straight to the computer, faithfully every morning by seven, in a ritual way, and by eight or so I have my writing almost done for the day. In this way I've written ten books in ten years. This writing time is a special time. I profit by sitting there every morning, working, trying, failing, succeeding. My biological clock has reset itself and I have switched from being a night person to a morning person.[166]

Eric Maisel—Writer

When I am working on a book or a story, I write every morning as soon after the first light as possible. There is no one to disturb you and it is cold and you warm as you write[167].

Ernest Hemingway—Writer

Late Night Creators

My favorite time is late at night. I seem to wake up and want to work after 10pm, in my bubble of night.[168]

Ed Askew—Painter, Songwriter

I work late at night. I'm awake and nobody bothers me. It's quiet and things come and talk to me in the silence.[169]

Diana Gabaldon—Author

Morning and Late-Night Creators

At seven o'clock in the morning I am already done with my friseur, and at seven I am fully dressed. Thereupon I compose until nine o'clock... I am in the habit (particularly when I come home early) of writing something before I go to bed. Frequently I forget myself and write till one o'clock,—then up again at six[170].

Wolfgang Amadeus Mozart —Composer

In the above examples, we see some creative people who use the morning period for their creativity, some who use the late-night period and one person, Mozart, who used both periods. But using both periods probably means we are not getting enough sleep which is not good for our health. Mozart did not live a long life. Although we cannot say with surety that lack of sleep contributed to his ill-health, it certainly didn't help. Frankly, either period—morning or late night—is good for finding solutions. As mentioned, the difference is going to bed early and waking up early is a healthier routine, which in the long run is better for our functioning as a solution system. Ill-health is a definite detriment for solving problems. People who are ill are not as productive as people who are healthy. Illness drains our energy and creativity requires energy. Illness also disrupts the orderliness of our consciousness. And without an orderly consciousness, it's very difficult if not impossible, to arrive at solutions.

Another aspect of our body clock is that most people have a wave of fatigue sometime in the afternoon. It could be 2, 3, or 4 p.m., again dependent on when we go to sleep, when we wake up, etc. If possible, we should take this afternoon wave of fatigue as an opportunity for a nap or a meditation to refresh ourself. The Spanish siesta is a tradition of napping during the afternoon fatigue time, not forgetting that the heat of the afternoon in southern climes is a contributing factor.

An excellent technique related to routine is to schedule creative activity at the same time every day. Just as we find if we go to sleep regularly at 10 p.m., around 9:45 p.m. we start to become sleepy, if we do our problem solving at a regular time, our consciousness becomes habituated to shift into a more alert state. Utilizing this scheduling procedure, we should combine sufficient sleep, our naturally lively mental times, and the power of habit. For most, it means creating in the morning. But for some, it means the late-night hours.

The environment in which we work also contributes to how well we solve problems. Noise, disturbances, and discomfort have an adverse effect on the orderliness of our consciousness. When we have to expend mental and physical effort to block out noise, disturbances, and discomfort, the effort as if acts as a barrier to our free flow of thoughts. The effort may also create fatigue which lowers our alertness, creativity, and intelligence. Therefore, it is advisable to have a quiet, comfortable, undisturbed environment for problem solving.

Unfortunately, this type of environment is rare. Many people even listen to music while they work. If the work is routine, our abilities are less affected and we may have the positive benefit that the music helps us stick to the task. But if the work requires serious mental exertion, music isn't the benefit people might assume. The primary reason people (often students) use music as a background to study or work is because they don't like the task and/or are anxious about it. Music makes it easier to begin the task and makes the time spent on the task more tolerable. Music may lift our mood and a happy mood does, to a degree, increase our alertness, creativity, intelligence, orderliness, and freedom, and any increase, however slight, is a good increase.

The difficulty is our consciousness moves in the direction of greater charm. This movement means, if we work with music in the background, our consciousness will constantly waver between the charm of the music and the charm—if there is any—of the task. Therefore, moments will occur when the charm of the task dominates and we won't even hear the music and moments will occur when the charm of the music dominates and we will not pay any attention to the task. Shifting between the work and the music or worse, at times fighting the music while trying to perform the task, is not the best situation. Our consciousness is better served by silence where it is not subject to this struggle. When we're working, we're telling our consciousness to work. By putting music on in the background, we're mixing signals. Our consciousness is trying to work but it's harder because our consciousness is constantly shifting to the absorbing music. Silence gives our consciousness one less object to become absorbed in. Of course, even in silence our consciousness drifts off when the task becomes dull (or when we have a charming idea or thought), but music only encourages and prolongs shifts, not to ideas and thoughts but to the music.

We've talked about how solutions come when we're shaving or traveling in a train or walking in the woods. But distractions in this context are not the same thing as our consciousness shifting back and forth between absorption in music and absorption in a task. When we come up with solutions when our consciousness is relatively free performing mundane tasks, it easily moves in the direction of a solution because it is NOT absorbed. Having our consciousness shift in the direction of greater charm when we are performing mundane, unimportant tasks is a good thing.

However, when we work, if we put on music, when our consciousness shifts to listen to the music, it's because the charm of the music is attracting our attention. In that attracted state, our consciousness is no longer free to shift in the charming direction of a solution. Music is designed to hold our attention. It's meant to absorb. When we're working, if a solution ever occurs when we have music on, it's because the music at least temporarily has failed in its goal of being charming—and our consciousness is then free to move in the direction of the solution. However, when we're working in a silent environment, our consciousness is not tempted by the music. Without music, we have one less hindrance on our path to solutions.

However, do not worry if we feel music is necessary. Anxiety can be a more severe block to solutions than music and background music may be the only way we can tempt ourself to work. Even if we begin the practice of meditation, it may take many months or even years before creating in silence is something we can tolerate regularly. However, if we have the choice, silence is preferred.

Painting, drawing, and sculpting—which deal with visual, spatial awareness as opposed to linear, logical, meaning-based reasoning—are some of the few problem-solving activities that background music interferes with less. When we're figuring out what a character in a play is going to say or calculating the answer to a physics problem or writing a report on why a new factory should be built, we're juggling words, concepts, and numbers in sequential, logical steps, and the intermittent absorption of music can make us lose our train of thought, creating a need for endless repeats and restarts.

Painting and sculpture require different mental muscles. When our consciousness uses visual, spatial thinking, juggling colors, shapes, sizes, and their relationships, we tend to deal with projects more as a whole. Even when we're manipulating a part, we see that part more as a visual whole rather than a logical sequence, and music does not seriously interfere with that form of non-linear thinking. In addition, music can stir the emotions and many will find that when operating with colors and shapes, a strong feeling level is a help. Nonetheless, silence is always preferred. Music constantly tugs at our consciousness for attention. Our consciousness arrives at all types of solutions best when it's free to move in the direction of greater charm, and for that experience silence—not absorbing music—is the ideal background.

In almost every instance, rest (in term of taking a break) is one of the best techniques for restarting a stuck consciousness. Here, we do not mean meditating, napping or sleeping. Every time we run into a mental block we cannot meditate, nap or sleep. We might not have the time or be in the appropriate setting. Meditating, napping, or sleeping are general techniques we should practice as part of our daily regimen, regardless of whether we are stuck on a problem or not. Here, by resting, we mean taking a short relaxing break such as chatting with an associate, or just pausing for a few seconds and staring off into space.

Pauses like these, for a few seconds or a few minutes, sometimes are enough to nudge our consciousness back into a solution state. It's analogous to what we do when a computer locks up. We shut the machine off, let everything reset and then turn the machine back on. In the same way, when we are stuck on a problem, if we rest even for a few moments, that short break may be enough to ease the strain or clear the fog, allowing our consciousness to reset and resume its flow.

However, while brief rests hold out the possibility of a fresh start, success from brief rests is infrequent. The deficiency in one or more of our qualities for solution is often too deep for a brief rest to restore. Nonetheless, brief rests in all their forms—pausing, talking, closing the eyes for a minute or two, etc.—are still good on-the-spot methods for restarting our consciousness.

While we've just mentioned obvious problems with napping or sleeping, recently, a study has appeared which suggests that a few minutes of very light sleep is an excellent way to enhance creativity.

> Renowned surrealist Salvador Dali had an unusual method of getting inspired. When he decided to take a nap on his chair after a long day of thinking about liquid watches and swans reflected in elephants (themes in his paintings) he would take a bunch of keys in his hand, place it on the edge of his chair and nod off in a light sleep. There was a metal tray on the floor and when he would really fall asleep, the keys would fall out of his hand, hit the tray with a loud noise and wake him up.

Like American inventor Thomas Edison, who used the same technique, Dali believed that sleeping this way gave him a creative boost. As soon as the object hit the tray, he would wake up and return to work. Many people think he was talented, but researchers only recently tested whether this technique will work even on people who aren't similarly gifted.

In a study published in *Science Advances*...researchers found that participants who spent at least 15 seconds in N1 [light sleep with non-rapid eye movement] tripled their chances of finding the hidden rule, implying increased creative thinking, than those who remained awake during the break. Eighty-three percent of people who entered the N1 sleep cycle were able to identify the rule compared to only 30% of the awake group.

"Here, we show that joint brain activity in the twilight zone between sleep and wakefulness (N1) ignites creative sparks," the authors stated, adding that "we believe N1 provides an ideal cocktail for creativity."

However, if they reached deeper sleep levels known as N2, monitored experimentally using an electroencephalogram, the effect passed.

The authors added that these results show that an incubation period, which is a short period of N1, has a significant effect on insight. But the beneficial effect disappears when people fall into a deeper sleep.[171]

What is interesting about this research into what we can call the "Edison-Dali technique" is that, as we've emphasized, the authors are not claiming that problems are solved during this light (N1) sleep but rather that the sleep state refreshes our consciousness to better enable it to solve problems, which is what we've been asserting. The other interesting point is that the article specifies that light sleep is the best refresher for the solution state and that it does not take a long time in this light sleep state for our consciousness to gain its needed refreshment. Interestingly, once the light sleep moment continues into deeper, duller levels of sleep, these deeper, duller sleep states are not as conducive to problem solving. The article does not claim that deep sleep states are not beneficial to our health, however, the research does emphasize that the best way to get a creativity boost is by spending a brief time in the lighter, more conscious (N1) sleep state.

The difficulty with the Edison-Dali technique is that it is so intricate. We have to fall into this light sleep and then immediately self-awaken by having a ball or a key or a similar object drop out of our hand into a pan that wakes us up. This series of conditions means that the technique is really only suitable for those who can nap easily and often, and whose hands will drop the held object soon after falling asleep and who will then be awakened by the dropped object. All these steps make the technique not only intricate but somewhat "bizarre," and probably not useful for all but a few and, even for those, only in special circumstances. Is an advertising executive who needs a solution by the end of the day going to be able to fall asleep—even a light sleep—sometime during that day in order to come up with his or her answer? We expect not.

However, the concept behind the technique is not without merit. Sleep does refresh our consciousness and put us in a better solution state. And their research concludes that the best type of sleep for this refreshment is a light sleep where consciousness is still, to a great degree, present and where brainwave activity is high. Thus, this research leads us to believe that the Transcendental Meditation technique is a far more practical and beneficial way to improve our problem-solving. Why go through all the convolutions of the Edison-Dali technique when with TM, we get a more powerful creative boost more easily and more dependably. During TM "EEG studies show (1) an increase in alpha 1 power in the frontal parts of the brain, and (2) an increase in alpha coherence in the prefrontal cortex"[172] (alpha waves are associated with N1 sleep which the "Edison-Dali" research finds so valuable). The TM technique only takes twenty minutes and works anywhere. Even an ad exec under the pressure of a deadline or a performer about to go on stage can do it. And TM not only produces the valuable alpha brain wave activity but also deep rest.

As a general rule, we don't practice TM at every instance of being stuck because with regular practice the positive effects last longer and longer during the day but an extra meditation can occasionally be done.

> Between dress rehearsal that we do and the live show that we do, I'll meditate [TM] in my dressing room from anywhere from 10 to 20 minutes; just to hone that muscle of being in the moment…[173]
>
> **Tom Bergeron—Former TV Host**
> **Dancing with the Stars**

> We went from the fall in Boston where it was nice and cozy to Los Angeles which was about 90 in the valley at the Los Angeles Zoo parking lot under a tent in a car under lights with the windows up and no air conditioning. It was about a thousand degrees in the car and

I had a monologue and I couldn't remember my lines. I knew that I knew them. I'd said them about a million times but I couldn't access them. They were completely lost in that wherever it goes and I could see all these poor grip guys sweating holding heavy equipment and they're looking at me like, get your lines right, woman, so we can get out of here and I realized, all of a sudden, I just need 25 minutes and I ran back to my trailer and I rebooted. I did my [TM] twenty-minute meditation and I came back and nailed it. It was like, we're done. Thank you very much. And we were out of there.[174]

Cameron Diaz—Movie Actress

Megan Fairchild, principal dancer for the New York City Ballet, does her TM before every performance, as does Tony award-winning actress Katie Finneran. So, does actor, singer, dancer Hugh Jackman, who says "I meditated before I hosted the Oscars. I meditate before I go onstage. I meditate in the morning and lunchtime when I'm on a film set. It's like it resets."[175]

Some recommend "creativity games and exercises" when stuck. Pretending to be an Einstein or a Newton and imagining looking at a problem as the genius would or repeating affirmative phrases such as "ideas are flowing to me" or "my mind is free" or "I am creative" attempt in a clumsy, superficial way to enhance one or more of the seven qualities for solutions. But the exercises most often involve mood making, manipulation, and force and therefore fail to increase, or even temporarily stimulate, any of the qualities for solutions.

Pretending we're an Einstein is not the same as being an Einstein. We do not have his level of consciousness and thus it's a mirage to try to mimic it. Similarly, exercises that require us to repeat phrases such as "My mind is free" or "Ideas are bubbling up through me" or that demand us to be more observant do nothing on the level of the physiology to increase our powers of observation or make our consciousness freer or increase our flow of ideas. As mentioned before, these techniques work only on the level of language or mood which is like a hungry man trying to convince himself that his stomach is full. Repetitions, affirmations, and moods are not a meal. They are delusions. The hungry man needs food and the problem solver needs greater alertness, creativity, intelligence, orderliness, freedom, information, and desire. At best, games, repetitions, and affirmations serve as interruptions from whatever work we are doing and, if not practiced intensely, can serve as a sort of pause or brief respite and, in that way, may help our consciousness restart. Games, repetitions, and affirmations can sometimes work as a psychological trick to get us to stop procrastinating and start in on a task, but they are not in themselves going to increase the seven qualities for solutions.

Some games and exercises show a better understanding of problem solving than others. Here, for example, is an exercise that attempts to induce a state of alertness and orderliness. It does not increase these qualities but, at least in theory, it tries to restore them. And unlike most games and exercises (albeit in a somewhat unusual way), it works on the level of the physiology.

1. Ring your bell loudly and shout, "Create!"
2. Feel the anxiety well up.
3. Gather your wits and say to yourself, "I know what to do."

199

4. Go to your workspace.
5. Set your kitchen timer for ten minutes.
6. If you're working on a book or building your home business web site, boot up your computer. If you're weaving, prepare your loom. Prepare to work.
7. Work for ten minutes.
8. When the timer, "bings," shout, "All clear!" (If you feel like working more, please do.)

> The drill is over. What you'll notice is that *a bucket of adrenaline* got activated just by announcing that it was time to create, but that *crossing to your work place in a deliberate way and matter-of-factly working settled your nerves.* The anxiety subsided and you could do what needed doing. Maybe you were still anxious; but you were also calm[176]. (emphasis my own)

Observe how in this exercise, it clearly states that part of the purpose of the exercise (the ringing of the bell) is to stimulate adrenaline—thereby creating alertness—and in the second part of the exercise, it is clearly stated that "walking.... in a deliberate way and matter-of-factly working settled your nerves," i.e., created a state of orderliness. Thus, the exercise does have, to some degree, an understanding of two of the seven elements required for solutions. It mimics the pressure of a deadline to increase adrenaline yet also attempts to maintain orderliness. The difficulty is that, as with the Edison-Dali technique, the method is so elaborate, it is not practical for frequent use, and even when it is attempted, it does not necessarily produce a deep enough level of alertness and orderliness to solve a problem and it certainly doesn't increase these qualities. But, in theory, in attempting physiologically to combine alertness and orderliness, the exercise demonstrates better insight into the creative process than most.

"Brainstorming," with another individual or in a group, is another technique for problem solving. The reason brainstorming sessions have value is because the group compensates for the weakness in each individual by utilizing the aggregate of the seven qualities for solutions that exist in the group. In other words, some individuals may have lower levels of orderliness or freedom or information but others may have higher levels of these qualities. Thus, the group as a whole balances each other's deficiencies and functions in total as a better solution system. But the key for a brainstorming session is for it to function freely and in a calm, cooperative manner.

Everyone in the group (even a group of two or three) must feel comfortable to contribute and everyone must listen to everyone else's ideas, otherwise the group is not drawing on its full value of the seven qualities for solution. In reality, no matter what the group's rules, whether formal or just understood, some individuals will dominate the group due to personality, popularity, appearance, articulateness, wealth, or position and reduce the contributions of others. As a result, the group will not function at full efficiency. Biases defeat the purpose of the group. If a group is to brainstorm successfully it must give all individuals a fair opportunity to speak, and prevent individuals from criticizing and ganging up on one another. Any individual can present more ideas than the others. He or she may have more ideas. But everyone must have a chance to contribute and everyone must consider all ideas without prejudice.

Human nature being what it is, a totally free, orderly group is probably as rare as a totally free, orderly individual but nonetheless that is the goal. Stipulating too many rules such as requiring everyone to speak or ensuring that one person does not speak more than others manipulates and controls the group and is potentially as harmful as having no rules. It is always a delicate balance between rules and freedom. Remember rules (order), can enhance freedom but too many rules can restrict freedom. Books on how to run a brainstorming session are plentiful. But whatever the specific approach, the goal should always be to maximize the free and orderly expression of ideas, so that the group as a whole produces the highest levels of the seven qualities for solution that exist in the group.

Since information is one of the seven qualities for solutions, information gathering is a vital technique for solutions and should not be practiced just while we are in school and then forgotten. Information gathering should be a constant part of our life, not only in areas of our main interests but in other areas as well. Solutions are based on connections, and knowledge from one field, no matter how tangential, may someday connect to another field, resulting in a brilliant *aha*. Michael Shane, a leading entrepreneur and proponent of information gathering, says, "Everyone is an information carrier. You never know who has that one piece of information you need." And it is true. Gather information every way possible. Always listen to others, from cab drivers to professors. We never know when someone will provide us with that one piece of invaluable information. Never stop gathering information and never ignore a possible source, no matter who, where, when, or what it is.

The importance of loving a subject cannot be overemphasized. Books on increasing creativity generally do not discuss desire except, perhaps, on the level of persistence, and often those discussions either overtly or covertly encourage focus, which is a form of control. We need persistence but persistence should still allow for taking breaks, getting a good night's sleep, meditating, and generally allowing our consciousness in some way to refresh itself. Also, books on creativity do not mention the deeper level of desire: the tendency of consciousness to flow in the direction of greater charm (i.e., the solution) and infrequently mention that our consciousness works best when we look for solutions in areas we love. Of course, we cannot always work in areas we love, but it's good to understand that loving a subject helps greatly when trying to solve problems. However, when our consciousness is fresh and alert, we naturally find greater enjoyment in whatever area we pursue—if we already love the subject, we love it more; if we do not love the subject, our increased awareness allows us to find greater pleasure in it. This increased capacity for enjoyment which a clear consciousness brings means that we can study a subject we don't like with greater vigor and persistence and our consciousness will flow more spontaneously and more precisely in the direction of solutions.

"Ahas" are elusive but they are always there. They lie deep in the pool of our consciousness. But when we are diving for those pearls, the clearer the pool, the deeper we can dive, and the easier the solutions are to see.

CHAPTER 21

Wakefulness and Genius

Thoughts flow one after the other like beads on a chain. But as effortlessly, quickly, and abundantly as our thoughts flow, solutions rarely occur in the same abundance. Only occasionally do we have moments where ideas flow in a rush and keep on flowing—but it does happen. Mozart wrote one of his greatest symphonies in less than a week.[177] Robert Louis Stevenson wrote the first draft of *Dr. Jekyll and Mr. Hyde* in three days.[178] Van Gogh painted some of his greatest masterpieces in one sitting. "During the last two months of his life in Auvers-Sur-Olse, Vincent completed a painting every day."[179] Such prodigious feats of creativity are possible whenever an individual's consciousness is at least temporarily clear and the individual's body is at least temporarily unexcited by stress. And if periods like this occur, it should be possible to stretch those periods into days, weeks, months, and years. Total wakefulness is what we want for everyone.

> The millions are awake enough for physical labor; but one in a million is awake enough for effective intellectual exertion, only one in a hundred million for a poetic or divine life. To be awake is to be alive. I have never yet met a man who was quite awake. How could I have looked him in the face?[180]
> **Henry David Thoreau—Walden**

Consciousness is the thinker. Consciousness is the creator. Consciousness is the solver. Pure consciousness is the field of total wakefulness and, by reaching pure consciousness, we can become wider and wider awake.

Tragically, every time some new crisis crops up, society looks not to consciousness but to information for salvation. Having no other method it recognizes or understands, society too often puts its faith in the limited field of information or as it is usually phrased: "learning about the problem." However, information by itself is never enough. Rather than devoting *all* of our attention to gathering every shred of data we can about a problem, we need to devote more time to developing the consciousness with which we connect the information. Ignoring the development of consciousness means whenever a new problem crops up, society is forced to wait for that one person in a hundred million who is awake enough to have his or her one in a million breakthrough, which leaves all human progress at risk.

Nonetheless, the world does have a history of geniuses propelling society forward. Although scattered thinly throughout society, geniuses do exist. Like a tree throwing out seeds in the hopes some will grow, nature provides that all over this planet, millions of individuals are born with different levels of consciousness, different types of physiologies, and different types of environments, so that in the many areas of human endeavor some precious few will have sufficient consciousness and resources to grow into magnificence. For instance, Mozart (one of the rarest of geniuses) was born with an extremely high level of consciousness, a physiology suited for music, and in an environment ideal for musical development. His father was not only a talented musician but a famous music teacher. The time period that Mozart was born into was fertile ground for music—his century had created and perfected musical instruments and ways to produce them at costs people could afford. Forte pianos which Mozart played were de rigueur for the best families. This was an age without movies, TV, radio, computers, and cell phones, but music was everywhere. It was a music mad age—either people playing sheet music at home by contemporary composers like Mozart, Hayden, and Beethoven or going to concerts and operas by the same composers and many others. Thus, as astounding as Mozart's feats of genius are, from a statistical point of view, his birth could almost be predicted.

But today we do not have to rely on statistics. Or, perhaps, more accurately we can say, statistically we can increase the odds of genius occurring. Since we are all conscious and can therefore reach pure consciousness, we can all improve our awareness. On an individual basis, it does not mean that anyone who regularly reaches pure consciousness will become a genius or even that anyone who regularly reaches pure consciousness will be better than his neighbor. It is not a competition. Everyone is born with a different level of consciousness. But it does mean that any individual who regularly reaches pure consciousness will be better than before he or she began. And if previously in every generation only one in one hundred million reached the heights of profound genius, with the knowledge and skill of transcendence that number will increase and more and more individuals will blossom into greatness. The spark of genius has never been missing from human life. What has been missing is the understanding of how to ignite it. The rush of ideas that before only came to us rarely can gradually become the dominant aspect of our life.

Does this mean that anyone who has sufficient degrees of all seven qualities for solving problems could, for instance, come up with the theory of relativity? The answer is a definite yes, if—and this is a big if—the person has sufficient degrees of the seven qualities for solutions. However, we need to understand what having these seven qualities present at sufficient degrees truly means. For example, let's look at information. As we've been explaining throughout this book, information is not just facts gleaned from books. Information is our whole life experience. It includes our education, relationships, recreation, work, memories, and thoughts.

Thus, anyone who truly has the same information as Einstein (not necessarily the exact same information but its equivalence) *as well as* the same degree of alertness, creativity, intelligence, orderliness, freedom, and desire could discover the theory of relativity. That level of equivalence is rare but it does happen. The history of science and invention is replete with such examples. Leibniz, a German philosopher and mathematician, invented Calculus at the same time as Newton. Elisha Gray and Amos E. Dolbear invented the telephone at the same time as Alexander Graham Bell. Alfred Russell Wallace formulated the principle of natural selection at the same time as Darwin. Joseph Wilson Swan invented the light bulb at the same time as Edison. These instances are not the only ones.

> In 1922, Ogburn and Thomas published some hundred and fifty examples of discoveries and inventions which were made independently by several persons, and, more recently, Merton came to the seemingly paradoxical conclusion that "the pattern of independent multiple discoveries in science is...the dominant pattern rather than a subsidiary one." He quotes as an example Lord Kelvin, whose published papers contain "at least thirty-two discoveries of his own which he subsequently found had also been made by others.[181]"

Art, of course, exhibits more individuality. No one else besides Melville is going to write *Moby Dick* and no one else besides DaVinci is going to paint the *Mona Lisa*. Other artists can be as good as Melville and DaVinci but artistic expression is more individualistic.

Mathematicians, physicists, and other types of scientists are focused on uncovering nature's laws. So, while the type of scientist they become is affected by their personality, their education, and their environment, their actual discoveries are open to duplication. Individualistic styles to how they work, how they write, how they explain will always exist, but the laws they discover will be universal which is why it is easier to site specific examples of simultaneous scientific discoveries than artistic expressions. Artistic expressions by definition are never going to be the same. A telephone can be invented by two individuals at approximately the same time. But two individuals are not going to compose the *Rhapsody in Blue*.

However, in the world of music, art, and literature, there is an equivalence. Many composers of Gershwin's time were also influenced by jazz and other aspects of their culture. Artists of the same period often have similar ideas about art and utilize similar styles to express them. We have Baroque music, Elizabethan poetry, Impressionist art, and Bauhaus architecture. Many artists of the same period contribute to these schools, and depending on the level of their seven qualities of solution, their art has more, less, or equal power. And when we look back in time on artists from the same school, their work can be mistaken for each other's, particularly by the non-expert. Thus, Hayden's music can be mistaken for Beethoven's and Renoir's painting can be mistaken for Monet's. But clear differences still exist in the actual art they create because of their differences as individuals.

And differences are always going to exist: genetic differences, economic differences, educational differences, environmental differences, etc. If we live in the desert, we may never learn to swim or how to sail a boat. If we have a terrible sense of smell or are hard of hearing, we may not develop the knowledge, skill, or desire to become a chef or a musician (Beethoven became deaf later in life after he had already mastered his musical skills). If we have a poor memory, it may hinder our ability to become a doctor. If we are color blind, we are unlikely to become a painter. It's not that weaknesses can't be overcome. It is that these factors seriously impact our choices and our skills—what we do, what we like, what we know, and what we create.

But wherever we are, whatever we are doing, and at whatever level of ability we are doing it, consciousness is the key. After all, Beethoven did not write masterpieces every day. Even though from day to day his genetic make-up, environment, education, likes and dislikes were the same, the state of his consciousness was always changing. His genetic make-up, environment, education, life experiences, etc. strongly influenced his musical skills, and how and what he composed, but at any given moment when he was composing, the state of his consciousness dictated whether he was stuck or inspired. The correct mix of the seven qualities for solution at the time we are working on a problem allows for or impedes *aha*s. Without the solution state, no solutions occur. Abundance is possible but we need the maximum wakefulness.

CHAPTER 22

The Benefit of Functioning as a Solution System for Relationships and Society

Relationships are most often judged by whether or not we like a person. If we like the person we are with, the relationship is good; if we dislike the person, the relationship is bad. Rarely do we evaluate a relationship in terms of the state of our consciousness. Yet, in reality, if we are with someone we like when we're worried, tense, and tired, our time together does not have the usual excitement and joy. Why? The person is the same. Our feelings for the person are the same, but when we are worried and tense, our ability to express our feelings is diminished. Our love does not flow. Maybe we behave curtly, lose our temper, and do not respond well to our friend's attempts to cheer us up.

In those situations, we usually find ourself apologizing by saying, "I'm sorry. I'm not myself," or "I'm out of sorts," or "This isn't me." And these expressions are correct. We are not our self. We are out of sorts. We are not "me." We are functioning from a level of a problem system—a level of worry, anxiety, and fatigue which is not the true nature of the self. The true nature of the self is clarity, confidence, and compassion. The true nature of the self is a solution system. But when we live as a problem system, bickering, arguments, and disagreements always occur. Just as the nature of a solution system is to create solutions, the nature of a problem system is to create problems.

An individual who functions as a problem system lacks inner contentment and therefore seeks in a relationship the inner happiness he or she is missing. Whenever two such individuals meet, with each looking to the other to fulfill his or her needs, the relationship is based on taking rather than giving and how can such a relationship last? A relationship based on taking is more vulnerable to failure because it is incapable of sufficient tolerance and sacrifice. Two individuals can never have all their desires coincide, so whenever their wants conflict, without the ability to give, difficulties arise. How can two individuals with high levels of need be patient and conciliatory? How can two individuals with high levels of need accommodate and adapt?

It's like a negotiation where one individual because of debt has to sell at a certain price, and the other because of a lack of capital has to buy at a certain price. Because of need, there is no flexibility, so they can never agree on a price. If there were less need or no need, compromise would be possible. So, in a relationship, if there is too much need on both sides, the capacity for compromise diminishes. Disagreements repeatedly occur and eventually the relationship collapses. If giving doesn't exist or only exists in small quantities, a relationship is destined to fail.

But if two people meet who have strong levels of inner satisfaction, they are fulfilled enough within so that giving overflows and their relationship naturally grows. Any relationship based on giving has more flexibility. Neither is forced to make demands the other can't fulfill or doesn't want to fulfill. If each individual is giving, at those times when their desires do conflict (which is going to happen occasionally no matter how alike they are), each will be more willing to accommodate and thus rather than discord, harmony will prevail.

We can only give what we are. We can only express what we are, and fundamentally what we are is our consciousness. A relationship is not two bodies or two personalities. It's the interplay of two consciousnesses.

Consciousness is the giver. Consciousness is the adorer. Consciousness is the lover. Depending on the quality of the consciousness of each person in a relationship depends the quality of the relationship.

Inner silence, inner contentment, inner happiness, inner orderliness is the key for positive, lasting relationships. But while a good relationship is a great foundation, it doesn't prevent disappointments, it doesn't prevent stress. Even good relationships have ups and downs, which means that a relationship cannot bring lasting fulfillment. If that is the goal of the relationship, it must fail. By failure, we do not mean the relationship must end; only that the relationship will not bring lasting happiness to our inner life. Relationships cannot even bring fulfillment in those rare instances when the relationship is good because one partner dies before the other. One partner may change over time in ways the other partner doesn't like.

This is not to denigrate the value of relationships. A relationship brings great happiness and contentment to the sweetest and tenderest levels of the heart. But it cannot bring true inner fulfillment. Although interestingly inner fulfillment always increases our ability to achieve better relationships because the greatest barrier to a good relationship is stress (disorder).

Orderliness is of paramount importance in a relationship. Orderliness allows for a harmonious relationship because each piece knows its proper place, and how and where they fit. Think of a set of gears. When the gears are synchronized, they mesh smoothly. When the gears are not synchronized, they clash, scrape, and fly apart. Order creates unity. Disorder creates disunity. If we meet someone, we do not want a hello one day and a growl the next. Erratic behavior creates stress. Orderliness does not mean monotony or drudgery or boredom. Order does not mean a lack of freedom, spontaneity, or differences. A good relationship is like a forest—a harmony of differences.

All throughout nature we see that two systems unite and remain united when they are orderly. Two systems never unite or, if they are united, break apart when they are disorderly.

> ...One of the amazing facts about electric charge is that there is an exact equality between the number of electrons and protons in the universe. If there were as much as one percent difference between the number of negative charges and positive charges inside one ounce of ordinary matter, this bit of matter would be torn asunder by a force equal to the total weight of the earth.[182]
> **Lloyd Motz—Author**

On every level of nature, we see that order creates unity; disorder creates disunity. When electrons order themselves around a nucleus, we have an atom. When planets order themselves around a star, we have a solar system. When bees order themselves around a queen, we have a hive. When people order themselves around a constitution or a monarchy, we have a nation. Every process of uniting requires orderliness and the most profound, yet simplest form of orderliness is love.

Love unites and order unites. Love harmonizes and order harmonizes. Love dissolves boundaries and creates oneness. Order dissolves boundaries and creates oneness.

When we are orderly, we are naturally more loving and when we are more loving, we are naturally more orderly. We see this correlation between love and order in how we interact with ourselves, others, and the environment. Those objects in our surroundings that we love, we take care of and keep clean and neat. Those objects we don't love, we neglect and let fall into disarray. Maybe our house is neat as a pin but our car is a mess or our office is tidy but our lawn is overgrown.

Even if we are a neat freak and are very paranoid about the physical appearance of everything, there are always aspects of our life we don't like that are in disarray (and we are not talking about things that are out of our control; we mean things that we could control if we wanted, but we don't because we don't want to). What we dislike, we ignore. What we like, we take care of. Even the messiest people always keep orderly those objects they love. Everything around them might be untidy but when it comes to the objects they care about—whether it's their kitchen, tv, garden, clothes, or work area—there we find neatness and order.

In our human relationships, we see the correlation between love and order even more clearly. In a family, although a mother always loves her children, when her consciousness is fresh and bright, i.e., orderly, that is when her love flows most spontaneously and that is when her children behave in their most coherent manner. They feel their mother's love, and even if they are in a mischievous or rambunctious mood, because their mother deals with them in a firm but loving manner they respond more promptly and more cheerfully. On the other hand, when a mother's consciousness is tired and tense, i.e., disorderly, her love flows less spontaneously. She is more likely to be impatient and sharp, and her children sense that, too, and become cranky and irritable. And since the mother's stressed times are when the children are most likely to misbehave and the mother is most likely to overreact, that is when chaos in the family grows. That is when yelling and door slamming starts. Unstable situations such as these produce much greater damage than we think.

For children, when a mother overreacts and punishes too harshly, the mother's overreaction is far more painful than any punishment. To children, their mother is the symbol of all that is good and just in the world.

> Mother is the name of God in the lips and
> hearts of little children.[183]
> **William Makepeace Thackery—Author**

And if their mother is unjust and disorderly, that means the universe is. If this injustice and disorder is continual and severe, it strikes deep into children's hearts, distorting their faith in the world, perhaps, for their whole lives. Moreover, when a mother punishes her children too harshly, she, too, is damaged by it. When a mother knows she is unfair to those she loves most, she is filled with guilt and remorse, increasing her own disorder. Yet a mother's disorderliness threatens all those who are close to her because the mother's role is to bind. The mother's role is to unite. The mother's role is to love. The mother's role is to be a solution system for the entire family.

When a mother does not function as a solution system, all of society is in danger because the family is in essence the seedbed of society. The family is where every individual grows. And when we have communities in which many individuals grow in harsh, unforgiving environments, we produce angry and undisciplined adults and a more uncivilized world. While, if the same individuals are raised in positive, caring environments, we create confident and considerate human beings and a more harmonious world.

The importance of the individual to the orderliness of society cannot be overemphasized. Like a family, every community is a collection of individuals living together in one geographical area. For the community to be orderly, sufficient numbers of individuals in the community have to be orderly.

For instance, contact between two people who are orderly naturally results in an orderly interaction. Contact between an orderly person and a disorderly person also is likely to result in an orderly interaction. It is difficult for a disorderly individual to excite an orderly individual unless the disorderly individual resorts to extremes of behavior which, due to the innate orderliness of consciousness, is relatively rare. That leaves as the primary contact for creating disorder, the meeting of two disorderly individuals; an event which mathematically is going to occur the least frequently.

Therefore, societies are fundamentally stable in that it's harder to create disorder than order unless we have a society in which a large number of disorderly individuals reside. Then, the odds of two such individuals meeting increases, and when two disorderly people confront each other, fireworks take place. If a society contains many such individuals, the resulting havoc spreads quickly. However, it takes a large number of disorderly individuals to create such violent societies which is a sad commentary on today since so many of our cities have vast areas where such extremes of violence exist.

For those living in disorderly areas, chaos is a constant part of life. The disorder of their physical environment conspires against them. The communities are usually densely populated, producing greater chances for conflict, which is why the level of fear in these areas is high. Since human beings require orderliness to grow and prosper little productive enterprise takes place. Businesses and services that can leave, do. The city or the areas of the city where the disorder seethes become increasingly dangerous and that only leads to more disorder. Yet, if we look at all the problems engulfing cities—crime, poverty, broken homes, illiteracy, and drug abuse—we see that they have one source: a disorderly consciousness. No matter how distant the problem may seem from the abstract field of awareness, a disorderly consciousness is the root cause of all social problems.

An individual with a disorderly consciousness is unable to attain an education or hold a job. If the individual can't get an education or hold a job, the individual can't alleviate his or her poverty. If the individual can't alleviate his or her poverty, the individual increases in disorderliness, which leads to more conflicts, drug abuse, and crime, which makes for more poverty. When we have such negative cycles occurring on a mass scale, we have a situation where entire communities plunge deeper and deeper into the abyss of problem systems constantly clashing with each other.

Governments try to help but their programs are most often ineffective. It doesn't matter what the country or what the area in the country, government programs do not treat the root. Government education and job training programs do nothing to transform people from within from problem systems to solution systems. Government education and job training programs only help those individuals who are already somewhat orderly and who can take advantage of the programs. But education and job training programs do nothing for the vast majority whose stress levels are so high they are unable or refuse to take advantage of whatever assistance is offered.

Other than receiving their daily ration of food, clothing, and shelter, they are so dull, angry, and suspicious they cannot behave in even a minimally acceptable manner. They cannot show up on time, conduct themselves courteously, or pay attention to what needs to be learned or done. And if they can't show up, if they can't pay attention, if they can't behave, if they can't learn, what good can an education or a job training program do? Who is going to hire individuals who function as problem systems and cause more trouble than they're worth? Dull, disorderly people are very difficult, if not impossible to educate no matter how excellent a nation's equipment and facilities are. Alert, orderly individuals soak up knowledge from whatever sources are available.

If we want to help individuals, we have to help them on the level of their consciousness, which on a practical basis is actually the easiest way to assist them and creates the greatest improvement to their level of awareness and their level of stress. Then, when they are mentally and physically calmer and clearer, they will spontaneously behave better, learn better, and work better.

Taking individuals from a high-crime area and moving them to a new housing development only results in another high-crime area. Removing gang members from the street and putting them in schools only produces dangerous schools. Recruiting the chronically unemployed and placing them in jobs only brings about inefficient workplaces—unless we transform these individuals from within from problem systems to solution systems. It is natural to want to grow and contribute to society. But first individuals have to think, speak, and act in a socially acceptable manner.

An example of the inadequacy of today's social programs are the measures governments take to alleviate criminal behavior. All over the world federal and state officials implement standard "rehabilitation programs" that never work. In these rehabilitation programs, criminals are confined to highly ordered environments, i.e., prisons, partly as punishment and partly in the hope that the criminal will absorb some orderliness from the disciplined life within the prison. In these strict environments, education and job training programs are offered to help the prisoner prepare for a better future. Unfortunately, life inside prisons is so stressful, prisoners increase in fear and anger more quickly than in knowledge and self-discipline. As a result, when they are released most commit more crimes. Recidivism rates in the US alone hover at 64%.[184] It may seem far-fetched to suggest that the way to eliminate criminality or juvenile delinquency is to teach highly disordered adults and teenagers to reach pure consciousness, but it is true.

To reach pure consciousness does not require orderliness. Orderliness is the result of reaching pure consciousness. To reach pure consciousness all an individual needs is the ability to think, and even the dullest, most disorderly individual can think. Here is one example of a prisoner's TM experience:

> I had tried everything and nothing had helped me, but I was still open to learn. I was instructed in the TM technique and after a few moments I experienced a slight weightlessness that was so beautiful… My mind became crystal clear… Suddenly I slipped into a level of consciousness that I had never experienced before. There seemed to exist nothing but a tranquil peace. When it was time to open my eyes, I could not help but notice how rested my body felt. Never had I felt so still and at ease…[185]

Even in jail, even when highly stressed, we can reach pure consciousness. A prison environment is not an obstacle to transcend. And the more prisoners we teach how to close their eyes and reach pure consciousness, the more prisoners who will transform themselves from within from problem systems to solution systems.

Here is an excerpt from a prison study done in the Oregon State Correctional Institution and the Oregon State Penitentiary.

> In this clinical trial, the TM technique showed significant reductions in TSC total trauma symptoms; anxiety, depression, the dissociation, and sleep disturbance subscales of the TSC; and in the Perceived Stress Scale relative to a usual-care control group. Results for the high-trauma symptoms subgroup indicated that the TM program might be particularly efficacious for those with higher levels of trauma symptoms....To our knowledge, this is the largest randomized controlled trial to date of the effects of the TM program on trauma symptoms, and the first of its kind conducted in a correctional setting. Prior studies have been conducted on veterans and international refugees in community-based settings and have found similar results in reductions in trauma symptoms because of TM practice. The current findings therefore build on prior gaps in the literature, extend the range of mental health benefits previously documented on the TM program, and provide further evidence for the clinical value of providing TM in correctional facilities and other institutional settings.[186]

Until we introduce the correct means to alleviate stress in the poor and the criminal, any hope of reducing poverty and crime is a dream. Unfortunately, the people in government who are responsible for solving social ills seem incapable of realizing this simple truth. Yet, if we look at the morass of today's problems, we can understand why. Experiencing pure consciousness is so innocent, so silent, so seemingly the opposite of the kind of urgent action we need. However, reaching pure consciousness is the only action that produces real change. Without it, problems multiply and display themselves in such complex and varied patterns, winding and twisting about each other, it becomes impossible to cut through the Gordian knot-like tangle and realize that the basic cause is the weakness in individual consciousness. With all the collective pain and suffering raging on the surface, it is difficult to understand that the answer lies deep below in the calm, clear, silent pool of consciousness.

CHAPTER 23

The Benefits of Functioning as a Solution System for the World

The farther out from a family we extend social relationships, the less love seems to play a role. For example, in work or in school, we don't think of love as playing an important part. But nonetheless love is still present and in a stronger way than we might think. It's very common in school to create strong bonds between schoolmates and to "love" a good teacher. At work, strong bonds are commonplace between employees and between employees and employers. Love for a city or a state is also part of our emotions. And love for our country is one of our strongest emotions. People even sacrifice their lives for their country.

In a crisis, an entire nation unites in a bond of love. For instance, in WWII, the United States bonded against a common enemy and, in a state of harmony, produced war materials at an unprecedented pace. Love of country served as a unifying influence and smoothed over many strikes and disagreements that otherwise may have disrupted the manufacturing process, not that strikes and political disagreements did not occur, but the overall feeling and practice was one of unity and the results of that unity were obvious.

> By a unanimous vote in the Senate and with
> the lone opposition of Rep. Jeannette Rankin

in the House, Congress declared war on the Axis powers, and most Americans quickly rallied behind the war effort. In the four years between the exercises at Ogdensburg and the invasion of Normandy, Americans came together en mass to raise, equip, transport, and feed a powerful Army and Navy that included 16 million men and 250,000 women. In total, 17 million men and women worked in war production plants, furnishing America and its allies with critical war matériel[187].

However, love does not always predominate in a country or in the world; internal disorder, when it is powerful enough, can overwhelm the influence of orderliness. For instance, today our planet is a giant problem system. Countries, cultures, and religions behave like heated molecules in a jar, bouncing, colliding, and smashing into each other. Disputes and armed conflicts occur frequently. We might think of the world as being at peace, since there aren't any major wars but we can pick almost any time, almost any continent, and find that conflicts rage. Below is a list from one recent year of a few of the countries engaged in conflicts. Names and locations change but the death and destruction never alters.

> Afghanistan
> Iraq
> Syria
> Yemen
> Somalia
> Nigeria
> South Sudan
> Ukraine
> Russia
> United States

Libya
India
Pakistan
Armenia
Azerbaijan
Ethiopia

Today our planet is so small and interdependent, every nation is affected by what every other nation does. Even countries that are not party to a conflict are in danger. Yet, despite the seriousness of the situation, governments persist in using outdated, ineffective methods to solve global problems—methods that have been tried for centuries and have always failed. Whether the solution is in the form of an alliance, trade agreement, treaty, or other pact, it almost never brings lasting peace. The reason is because even on a global level, the root cause of conflict is a weakness in consciousness.

Any nation is a collection of individuals and the level of consciousness of the nation is the aggregate of the level of consciousness of the individuals. As the mass of individuals feel, think, and act, so does the nation. When two nations have a dispute such as a border dispute, it is never the dispute that is hard to resolve. Borders are lines on a map, lines can be moved, resources shared, dual nationalities created. Endless solutions are possible. Where the intransigence lies is in the disorderliness that exists within the consciousness of the people, preventing the implementation of such solutions.

When the level of consciousness of two nations is weak, no solution quells the mistrust that each side feels toward the other. Compromise is difficult because each side is afraid, and when and if an agreement is reached, fear makes each side ready to pounce on the other. However, if the level of consciousness of the two nations is strong, any just and equitable plan allays the anxiety of the people and the solution is lasting because an alert, orderly society is less subject to fear. Solutions between calm, coherent societies are simple to reach. Solutions between angry, incoherent societies are very difficult if not impossible to reach. Yet, rather than work on the level of consciousness and produce alert, intelligent, creative individuals who easily accept any fair solution, international bodies try to bring together groups of angry, confused, discontented individuals who have great difficulty creating an agreement and an even greater difficulty abiding by it.

Even in the midst of a crisis like a war, it may seem hard to believe that the solution is to reach pure consciousness but it is true. It is the very difficulty we have believing in this solution that is such a large part of the problem. But even in war, soldiers sleep. Even in war, government leaders sleep. Even in war, civilians sleep. And, if during a war, they can close their eyes to sleep, they can close their eyes for a few minutes longer to reach pure consciousness. Then, when they open their eyes, soon there will be no more war.

Will peace happen by magic? No. Will peace happen overnight? In a week? Probably not. A month? Three months? Perhaps. But whatever the time span, it will happen. It will happen because the anger and fear of the constituents of the two nations will soften and the idea will surface that war isn't necessary; that differences can be settled peacefully. The idea will spread. Perhaps, a peace movement will spring up within one or both countries. Newspapers will print editorials advocating peace. Soon the leaders of both countries will feel that peace presents a better opportunity to achieve their goals than war. The exact path to the peace is irrelevant. It doesn't matter how talks unfold but a cease-fire will result. Peace can occur through many different avenues. Peace can occur quickly or slowly, depending on how stressed the people are and how many begin the practice of regularly reaching pure consciousness. But what is important is that somehow, someway, cooler (more orderly) heads will prevail because in the consciousness of the individuals will be more clarity and coherence and those qualities are the building blocks of peace, not war.

We might object that terrorists will never learn to reach pure consciousness and therefore it is a useless remedy for that form of violence. But terrorists survive within the context of a much larger society. It is from this larger community that they receive their support. For this larger community to consider terrorism as a cure for their ills, its consciousness must be permeated by anger, fear, and hatred. Such a society is as if shackled by its own stress. Yet, we have seen that even in prison individuals can reach pure consciousness. And once individuals experience the peace, tranquility, and clarity of pure consciousness, those individuals will no longer support terrorism. Just as it only takes a small light to dispel darkness, it only takes a few individuals to begin changing a society from negativity to positivity. And once the light is lit, more and more individuals will see the truth. We can go over and over this reasoning but no matter what form of human cruelty or ignorance prevails, the root cause is always a weak, disorderly consciousness.

When two individuals with a disorderly consciousness confront each other, we have a fight. When a few hundred or a few thousand confront each other, we have a riot. When millions confront each other, we have a war. Treaties are always possible but they are temporary solutions. When the vast majority have a tense, chaotic consciousness, violence lurks. The only true and permanent solution is to eliminate the root cause of violence which is a weakness in awareness.

As the philosopher/poet Lao-Tzu writes:

> The way to use life is to do nothing through acting,
> The way to use life is to do everything through being.

When a leader knows this,
His land naturally goes straight.
And the world's passion to stray from
   straightness
Is checked at the core
By the simple unnamable cleanness
Through which men cease from coveting,
And to a land where men cease from coveting
Peace comes of course.[188]

It has long been believed that the failure to solve national and international problems is the fault of governments. That belief is wrong. How can a government create solutions if the consciousness of its citizens function on the level of disorder? Disorderly people resist all change, disobey all regulations, and fail to carry out even the simplest tasks correctly. If stress exists so strongly in a nation that its citizens cannot create order in their own lives, how can their government rely on them to instill order in their country?

It doesn't matter what the form of government— whether it's democratic, communistic, socialistic, dictatorial, or monarchical—if its citizens function as problem systems, the country will remain mired in problems. For thousands of years, this planet has witnessed innumerable forms of governments. Even today, somewhere on this planet are governments of every stripe and description, yet nowhere on this planet does a government exist that is creating a society that functions on the level of solutions. Nowhere on this planet is there a government helping all its citizens live prosperous, happy, fulfilled lives. While it is true that some governments perform better than others, is that the result of the type of government or is it the result of the consciousness of the governed? Different types of governments might be better or worse as systems, but one thing is sure: no government can succeed if its citizens function as problem systems; while any government can prosper if its citizens function as solution systems.

We might wonder: How can a bad form of government such as a brutal dictatorship govern a country effectively? Yet, in reality, if we have a country that consists of citizens who are operating as solution systems, a brutal dictatorship is impossible. Governments do not spring out of nowhere and subjugate people. Governments grow out of the consciousness of the governed and the needs of the times. When the consciousness of the citizens of a country is dull and disorderly that is fertile ground for a dictatorship. The dullness of the citizens invites subjugation and their disorderliness makes the imposition of order by force more likely and sometimes even necessary.

Throughout history we see dictatorships arising most often in countries where the population is uneducated and unruly; while democracies and republics arise most often in countries with, at least, a nucleus of educated, orderly citizens. In those few instances where dictatorships emerge in alert, well-educated, orderly societies, it is due to severe crises like a war or a depression, and when the crisis is over, the dictatorships are soon overthrown.

The mistaken view is, if a government is inefficient and incompetent, all the nation has to do is change the government. Yet how often do we see countries where the government, either by revolution or by election, changes but the problems remain the same. To truly change a country, the consciousness of the people has to change. Citizens of a country should not blame their government. If their nation has problems, they should blame themselves.

Every government reflects the consciousness of its citizens in the same way that our individual consciousness reflects the coherence or incoherence of our body. Wherever well-educated, orderly individuals exist in large numbers, an efficient, effective government and a prosperous nation arises. Wherever uneducated, disorderly individuals exist in large numbers, a wasteful, corrupt government and a poor nation follows.

That a government reflects the consciousness of its citizens is evident in that all over the world people want honest governments, yet no matter where we look dishonesty permeates every aspect of government. Why? Because dishonesty permeates every aspect of society and every government is made up of the people of society. To the degree that dishonesty exists in the people, it exists in the government. Yet the steps we take to correct this dishonesty are ridiculously superficial. We don't strike at the cause. We don't try to transform the consciousness of the people from dull and disorderly where they are easily tempted, to strong and coherent where temptation is resisted. Instead, we act on the level of the symptoms. We focus on each instance of wrong doing and create new laws to prevent that specific form of misbehavior.

Too many politicians taking bribes, we pass laws against bribes. Too many politicians being influenced by special interest groups, we limit how much money groups can contribute. Too many politicians staying in office too long and misusing their power, we restrict how many times a politician can be elected. And, perhaps, the new rules and regulations succeed in preventing some instances of abuse. But as soon as one abuse disappears, another immediately takes its place.

Why?

Because laws cannot create a change in consciousness. And when an object such as money exists that human beings covet, then human beings will make every effort to achieve that object. Laws can never eliminate illegal behavior. There are not enough laws in the universe nor enough legal institutions to enforce them to prevent some individuals from getting what they want, legally or illegally. Ways around laws will always be found if the reward for breaking or sidestepping those laws is great enough. The solution to corruption is to have citizens who are not corrupt—citizens who function on the level of solutions and who gain their desires honestly.

When the citizens of a country are honest, the government is honest. When sufficient numbers of individuals in a country act in an ethical manner, the power of their honesty increases tenfold. It is much easier to be honest in a society where many people are honest than in a society where many people are corrupt. People are greatly affected by what others think and do. No one wishes to be shamed publicly. So, if a great many people are ethical, it is difficult for any citizen to take a bribe. If very few citizens take bribes, it becomes a tradition, and once it's a tradition, it's instilled into the moral fiber of the country and serves the nation for generations. On the other hand, if a great many citizens are dishonest, it's easy for everyone to be dishonest, and once that becomes a tradition, it, too, is infused into the moral fiber of the country and cripples the country for centuries.

Governments make easy scapegoats. They are like the coaches on an athletic team. When the team does badly, the easiest solution is to fire the coach. He's only one person. The owner can't fire the entire team. Likewise, when a country has problems, the easiest solution is to change the government. Who can change the entire population?

Yet that is the point. Until the population changes, the government is not going to change. Changing the names and personalities of government officials might be superficially satisfying but it is not going to create real change. A new government might be different. It might be a government of the right or the left or the center but it will be equally ineffective unless the citizens of the country change. Governments reflect change. They do not cause it. For real change to take place, it has to take place on the level of the consciousness of the people. And to make a real change in the consciousness of the people, each person has to take it upon him or herself to reach pure consciousness. Once that task is accomplished, each individual in the country improves, and as more individuals improve, the entire country grows in creativity and productivity.

Of course, there are those who dismiss incompetent and immoral governments as the root cause of world problems. They insist the root cause of suffering is economic. They say, if only we improve the economic condition of every country, we can eradicate crime, poverty, and war.

But how do we improve the economic conditions of a nation?

Wealth lies in a country's natural resources: its farm land, its raw materials, its geographical location, and most importantly, its citizens. If the citizens of a country are weak, a country always remains impoverished no matter what natural resources it has. Or at best, its wealth winds up in the hands of a few, while the majority of the population languishes in poverty.

Wealth doesn't create individuals who function as solution systems. Pure consciousness creates individuals who function as solution systems. Wealth is the result of solutions, not the cause. We can observe this verity in the high rates of drug abuse, alcohol abuse, suicide, and divorce that exist among the wealthiest citizens of the wealthiest nations because wealth has not brought these individuals the ability to solve all their problems. While the wealthy are creative and intelligent enough to gain, maintain, and increase their wealth, they are not creative and intelligent enough to function completely as solution systems. Stress and tension still infect their lives.

Even though this truth is easily gleaned from the lives of the wealthiest who sip from the cup of the world's most extravagant pleasures, we still cling to the fallacy that objects can create permanent happiness.

The wealthiest learn this lesson the hard way. They obtain so many objects of their heart's desires, yet despite that gain, nothing about their internal life changes. They are the same individuals they always were. At the center of all their happiness is still hollowness. This realization is the beginning of a terrible despair for what is more terrible than attaining one's heart's desires and having the happiness from that attainment fade into nothingness after a day, a week, a month, a year? And then what? Then what? Then what?

As Winona Ryder, a film actress who achieved considerable success when young, relates:

> I was driving and it was in the middle of the night. I was feeling depressed… I was very lonely. I was living in LA and…things weren't going well and I passed a magazine stand and I was on the cover of I think *Rolling Stone* and it said, "Winona Ryder, The Luckiest Girl In The World" and it had this picture of me and I was just going, I don't feel like the luckiest girl.—I felt like I didn't know who I was…[189]

At this time, Winona Ryder was suffering from so much pain and confusion she checked into a mental hospital.[190] Yet, according to conventional values she had everything. Beauty. Talent. Success. Wealth. Fame. Power. Youth. But it was not enough to avoid loneliness. It was not enough to eliminate unhappiness and despondency. And it certainly was not enough, later in life, to avoid drug and legal problems. Which is not to pick on Winona Ryder. She has grown as a person and continues her success.

But every day the tabloids are full of the problems of celebrities who, by all accounts, have everything good that life can offer. And even though very few of us are movie stars and land on the cover of *Rolling Stone*, we all have achieved some long-sought desire and then been shocked and dismayed at how quickly our joy disappeared. It is a universal disappointment because, once the exuberance from the achievement of transient desires wanes, we are left with no other choice but to chase after more desires, wondering where is the permanent fulfillment we seek. But the satisfaction gained from transient goals is always transient. Although nature dictates that objects and experiences change and fade, it is hard to break the illusion that material objects bring lasting happiness

Desires are important. Desires are the motivating force of life. But desires are endless and the happiness gleaned from achieving material objects all too quickly vanishes. To achieve lasting happiness, we have to gain our inner desire: pure consciousness.

And if per chance we view the world in scientific terms and think technology is the key to creating a problem free society, that view, too, is unsatisfactory. Neither technology nor its lack eliminates problems. Certainly, we can look at some technologically primitive countries and see that their slower lifestyle brings relief from many modern ills such as hypertension and heart disease. However, that appealing picture takes on a bleaker hue when we observe the poor hospitals, sanitation, and food production that accompanies their technological backwardness. While for those of us living in scientifically advanced countries, we know too well technology's darker side.

Pollution ravages the land to such an extent that it is now possible to imagine the destruction of our entire planet. Rather than having the means to chop down a tree or dam a small stream, technology gives us the power to destroy entire forests, rivers, lakes, and oceans. And if through technology we manage not to devastate our planet, the increasing levels of stress we toil under has brought us to the brink of destroying ourselves. We work too hard, drive too fast, fly too far, and move too often. Newspapers, radios, TV's, and the Internet barrage and bewilder us with real and fictional horrors. We are allergic to the chemicals we put in our clothes, houses, and food; we kill and maim ourselves with cars, motorcycles, and guns; we create drugs that cure one disease and cause ten; we manufacture weapons of mass destruction and use them; we destroy practically everything on this planet that grows, breathes, and feels.

In short, technology is out of control. Or is it we who are out of control? Isn't the real problem that our consciousness is creative and intelligent enough to produce technological advances but is not creative and intelligent enough to use those advances to help our planet rather than destroy it?

> The unleashed power of the atom has changed everything save our modes of thinking and we thus drift toward unparalleled catastrophe.[191]
> **Albert Einstein—Physicist**

What we need is to master the age-old technology of reaching pure consciousness and thereby bring our thinking into harmony with nature. Technology does everything except teach us how to properly use technology. That is the domain of consciousness, and until we expand our consciousness, technology will always be a two-edged sword, destroying as much as it creates.

It is not governments, wealth, education, or science that produces a problem free society. It is consciousness. If we live our lives as problem systems, problems increase on all levels;

while if we live our lives as solution systems, solutions on all levels multiply.

True change has to be on the level of the individual and true change for the individual has to be on the level of consciousness. Then, it is easy for ourself and the world to improve.

Our fate is not destiny, it is our choice. And everyone chooses. We do not need to blame our parents, neighbors, boss, mayor, or president. Everyone on this planet chooses whether to function as a problem system or a solution system. The choice is purely an individual choice and the actions needed to change from a problem system to a solution system are purely individual. And whichever way we choose—to function as a solution system or a problem system—we reap the consequences. The responsibility is our own. The capacity for acting as a solution system is within the grasp of everyone. It is embedded in our consciousness from birth for us to use or ignore.

How many individuals does it take to change society? Does every individual have to change before all of society changes? If a city has ten thousand people, does every person have to live as a solution system before the influence spreads throughout the populace? Individuals both influence and are influenced by their friends, their associates, their community, their state, their country, and their world. If fifty percent of a population act as solution systems will the entire nation prosper? Will the economic, technological, and educational systems improve, so that the life of every individual blossoms and everywhere health, harmony, and peace reign? And if that happens, perhaps, with fifty percent, can it happen with forty, thirty, ten or only one percent?

It is like Abraham bargaining with God for the survival of Sodom and Gomorrah. How many righteous (orderly) people does it take for society to survive? How many righteous (orderly) people does it take for society to flourish? God settled with Abraham on ten righteous (orderly) people for the survival of Sodom and Gomorrah out of a population that may have numbered in the thousands but, unfortunately, Abraham couldn't even find ten righteous people and the two cities were destroyed. Let's hope, today, sufficient numbers of individuals, whatever the true percentage may be, take the responsibility to function as solution systems, so that on this planet we not only survive but grow into the kind of wide-awake individuals we are capable of becoming, and as fully awakened individuals, fashion the ideal world we are capable of creating.

FINIS

BIBLIOGRAPHY

1   Hans Mersmann, Editor, Letters of Wolfgang Amadeus Mozart (New York: Dover Publications, 1972, preface p. vii)
2   Brewster Ghiselin, The Creative Process, (Berkeley, University of California Press, 1952) p. 110
3   Brewster Ghiselin, The Creative Process, p. 174
4   Andre Previn, The Story of the Symphony, Video Letter Quoted from Ludwig Van Beethoven
5   Arthur Koestler, The Act of Creation (New York: Penguin Books, 1989, p. 117)
6   Graham Wallas, The Art of Thought, 1926
7   Brewster Ghiselin, editor, The Creative Process, p. 27
8   Ralph Lewis, M.D., What Actually Is a Thought? And How Is Information Physical? Psychology Today, February 24, 2019
9   Gerald M. Edelman, Consciousness, R. R. Donnelly & Sons, 2004, p. 8
10 Sign in Toscanini's Ice-Cream Store, Cambridge MA, November 20, 2002
11 Frances Sheridan Goulart, The Caffeine Book, (Dodd, Mead & Company p. 11)
12 Ibid
13 Yom, Wikopedia, Internet
14 Abiodenesis, Wikopedia, Internet
15 Heat Energy, Science Learning Hub Internet, Nov. 20th 2009
16 Theory of Everything, Wikipedia
17 Consciousness, Gerald M. Edelman, R. R. Donnelly & Sons, 2004, p. 8
18 Richard Holloway, God's Priorities for Your Life for Teens, p. 307
19 Frans van Houten, Brainyquotes online website
20 Max Planck, A Survey of Physical Theory, p. 76
21 Michio Kaku and Jennifer Thompson, Superstrings: A Theory of Everything?, (p.4)
22 David Rudd Cycleback, Ockham's Razor and the Principle of Simplicity, Cycleback.com

[23] Ernst Mach, The economical Nature of Physics, in Popular Scientific Lectures, trans. Thomas J. McConnack, 1910 p. 197

[24] David Rudd Cycleback, Ockham's Razor and the Principle of Simplicity, Cycleback.com

[25] Francois Truffaut, Hitchcock, (New York: Simon and Schuster, 1967, p122)

[26] Fascinating Rhythm: The Collaboration of George and Ira Gershwin, (p.93)

[27] Antoine de Saint-Exuperey, Goodreads Online

[28] Hunter S. Thompson (2012). "Ancient Gonzo Wisdom", p.205, Pan Macmillan

[29] Voltaire (2016). "Voltaire—Premium Collection: Novels, Philosophical Writings, Historical Works, Plays, Poems & Letters (60+ Works in One Volume)—Illustrated: Candide, A Philosophical Dictionary, A Treatise on Toleration, Plato's Dream, The Princess of Babylon, Zadig, The Huron, Socrates, The Sage and the Atheist, Dialogues, Oedipus, Caesar...", p.4095, e-artnow

[30] Ralph Waldo Emerson, Ralph Waldo Emerson, Barbara L. Packer, Joseph Slater, Douglas Emory Wilson (2003). "The Conduct of Life", p.154, Harvard University Press

[31] John Ciardi, How Does a Poem Mean? (p.775)

[32] Post-Bernstein, Robert and Michelle, The Sparks of Genius. (Houghton-Miflin, Boston, 2001) p. 76

[33] Need to find this physics reference

[34] Arthur Beiser, Physics, Third Edition, (Reading, MA: The Benjamin Cummings Publishing Company, Inc. p. 351)

[35] Hans Mermann, The Letters of Wolfgang Amadeus Mozart, preface p. vii

[36] Albert Rothenberg And Carl Hausman, Editors, The Creativity Question, (Durham, North Carolina: Duke University Press, 1976, p. 66)

[37] Ibid, p. 66-67

[38] Graham Wallas, The Art of Thought, (London, C. A. Watts & Co. 1926) p. 53

[39] Willis Harman & Howard Rheingold, Higher Creativity, (Jeremy P. Tarcher, Los Angeles, 1984), p. 58

[40] Rosa Newmarch, The Life and Letters of Peter Ilich Thaikovsky, (new York, Haskell House Publishers, 1970) p. 274-275

[41] Kojiro Tomita, Goodreads Quotes Online

[42] Maria Montessori, The Secret of Childhood, chapter 8, p. 52

[43] Bertrand Russell, The Conquest of Happiness, 1930

[44] Robert Southey, The Creative Brain, Ned Herman Brain Books, p. 87

45 Maria Montessori, The Discovery of the Child, Ballantine Books, 1986, p. 84

46 Dmitri Ivanovich Mendeleev, Mendeleev on the Periodic Law: Selected Writings, 1869-1905

47 Henri Poincare, Science and Method, Cosimo, Inc., Jan 1, 2010,p. 22

48 Angels in Judaism, Wikipedia

49 Hierarchy of Angels, Wikipedia

50 Bill Veeck, Goodreads quotes, Internets

51 Arthur Koestler, The Act of Creation, p. 381

52 Unknown, Jackson Pollock, p. 182

53 Jackson Pollock: Meaning and Significance, Claude Cernuschi, (New York, Harper Collins, 1992) p. 115

54 Irving Stone, Editor, Dear Theo, (New York: Signet Penguin Book, 1969) p. 391

55 Carl Nordenfalk, The Life and the Work of Van Gogh, (New York: Philosophical Library, 1953) p. 143

56 Ibid, p. 172

57 Irving Stone, Editor, Dear Theo, p. 412

58 Tony Hillerman, Coyote Waits

59 Jose Saramago, The Double

60 Aaron Sorkin, The West Wing Script

61 James Gleick, Chaos Theory, (Penguin Books, New York, 1987)

62 Francois Truffaut, Hitchcock, Simon & Schuster, p. 52

63 Sharon Begley, Why Our Brains Love Horror Movies: Fear, Catharsis, a Sense of Doom, Daily Beast, 2017

64 Gayle Forman, brainyquote.com/topics/catharsis

65 Laura van den Berg, brainyquote.com/topics/catharsis

66 Richard Morris, The Edges of Science, Prentice-Hall, New York, 1990, p. 25

67 David P. Barash, Over Time, Buddhism and Science Agree, Nautilus, Internet Magazine, 2014

68 NASA Science, Share the Science, Supernovae Leave Behind Neutron Stars or Black Holes, Internet Magazine

69 Brewster Ghiselin, Editor, The Creative Process, p. 26-27

70 John Koch, The Interview, Gianfranco Zaccai, (The Boston Globe Sunday Magazine, The Boston Globe, May 11, 1998) p. 10

71 Brain book p. 271

72 Amy Fries, "Aha" moments Caught on Tape, Psychology Today

73 Liza Mundy, Code Girls: The Untold Story of the American Women Code Breakers of World War II, Hatchett Books

[74] Ned Herrmann, The Creative Brain, (Brain Books, North Carolina, 1989) p. 271

[75] Ibid, p. 118

[76] Maltz, Maxwell, Psycho-Cybernetics, Pocket Books, 1969, p. 81-82

[77] Albert Einstein, QuotePark.com, Internet Online

[78] Mick Jagger, Howard Stern Show Radio Interview, September 29, 2021

[79] Concise Columbia Encyclopedia, Columbia University Press, 1995

[80] Plato, ION, The Dialogues of Plato, translated by Benjamin Jowett, (Great Books of the Western World, Encyclopedia Britannica) p. 144

[81] Silvan Areisti, Creativity: The Magic Synthesis, (New York: Basic Books) p. 3

[82] Homer, The Odyssey, translated by Robert Fitzgerald, Farrar, Strauss and Giroux, New York, 1998, Book 1, Page 1

[83] John Milton, Paradise Lost, Book 1, Page 1

[84] Harriet Hyman Alonso, Yip Harburg Legendary Lyricist and Human Rights Activist, (Wesleyan University, 2012

[85] Aaron Copeland, What to Listen for in Music, Mentor Books, 1953, p. 23

[86] Howe, Julia Ward, Reminiscences, Houghton, Mifflin: New York, 1899. p. 142

[87] Robert Herrick, Delight in Disorder, Poetry Foundation, Online

[88] Olivier Wecxsteen, Sightlines, (Boston Ballet Magazine, volume xii, number 1, October 1966) p. 4

[89] Rollo May, The Courage to Create, 1975, p.119

[90] Lynch, David, Catching the Big Fish, (Tarcher/Penguin 2006), p. 111

[91] Michael Caine, Acting in Film, (Applause Theater Book Publishers, 1990) p.29

[92] Sara Pot, Moving Easy in Harness, Christian Courier Online, Sept 11, 2016

[93] Igor Stravinsky, An Autobiography, (M. & J. Steuer, New York, 1958) p. 20

[94] Igor Stravinski, An Autobiography, (M. & J. Steuer, New York, 1958) p. 151-152

[95] Maria Montessori, The Absorbent Mind, p. 204

[96] The Art Story Contributors, Vincent Van Gogh Artist Overview and Analysis, theartstory.org/artist/van-gogh-vincent/artworks, Jan. 2012

[97] Arthur Koestler, The Act of Creation, p. 124

[98] Jerry Seinfeld, Howard Stern Show, Howard Stern Interview, 5-24-2020

[99] John Koch, Butch Hobson Interview, Boston Globe Magazine, July 9, 1994

[100] Karl Iglesias, Insider Secrets From Hollywood's Top Screen Writers, Adams media, New York, p. 129

[101] Vincent Van Gogh, BrainyQuotes, Internet

[102] Steve Jobs, Stanford University Commencement Speech, June 12, 2005

[103] Tom Rath, Brainyquotes, Online Website

[104] Alexandra Johnson, The Hidden Writer: Diaries and the Creative Life, (New York: Doubleday)

[105] Jaffer Ali, Being "In the Zone," Shelley Palmer Blog, Nov. 1, 2012

[106] Jaffer Ali, Being "In the Zone," Shelley Palmer Blog, Nov. 1, 2012

[107] Jaffer Ali, Being "In the Zone," Shelley Palmer Blog, Nov. 1, 2012

[108] Andy Nesbitt, Bill Belichick Quoting from Art of War, usatoday.com, Nov. 25, 2019

[109] Michael O. Schroeder, What Is Lucid Dreaming? US News Oct. 25, 2018

[110] Kendra Cherry, The Four Stages of Sleep, Verywellhealth, online, July 9, 2021

[111] Brewster Ghiselin, editor, The Creative Process, p. 27

[112] Bertrand Russel, Portraits from Memory and Other Essays, (New York: Simon and Schuster, 1956) p. 211-212

[113] Isaac Goldberg, George Gershwin: A Study in American Music, (New York: Frederick Ungar Publishing, 1931) p. 139-140

[114] Brewster Ghiselin, The Creative Process, p. 111

[115] Graham Greene, The End of the Affair, Heinemann, 1951

[116] Arthur Koestler, The Act of Creation, p. 153

[117] Merriam Webster Dictionary, 1974

[118] Arthur Koestler, The Act of Creation, p. 116-117

[119] Albert Rothenberg and Carl Hausman, The Creativity Question, p. 63

[120] William C. Dement, Ph.D., The Promise of Sleep, p. 319, (Delacorte Press, New York, 1999)

[121] J. Allan Hobson, M.D., The Chemistry of Conscious States, (Boston, Little, Brown and Company, 1994) p. 72

[122] Angela Duckworth, BrainyQuotes Online

[123] Shelly Gable, Elizabeth A. Hopper, Jonathan w. Schooler, When the Muses Strike: Creative Ideas of Physicists and Writers Routinely Occur During Mind Wandering, PubMed, Jan. 17, 2019, Vol 30, Issue 3, pages 396-404

[124] Daniel Golden, (Boston Sunday Globe Magazine, January 14th, 1996) p. 7

[125] J. Allan Hobson, M.D., The Chemistry of Conscious States, p. 28

[126] Hans Mersmann, Editor, The Letters of Wolfgang Amadeus Mozart, p. 39-40

[127] Anthony Trollope, Autobiography of Anthony Trollope, (New York: Oxford University Press, 1980) p. 175-176

[128] Brewster Ghiselin, Editor, The Creative Process, p. 193-194

[129] Ibid, p. 49

[130] Irving Stone, Editor, My Dear Theo, p. 361

[131] Rosa Newmarch, The Life and Letters of Peter Ilich Tchaikovsky, p. 274

[132] Willis Harman & Howard Rheingold, Higher Creativity: Liberating the Unconscious for Breakthrough Insights, p. 58

[133] Helen Palmer, editor, Inner Knowing, from chapter 25, Intuition, by Arthur Deikman, (Jeremy P. Tarcher/Putnam, New York, 1998, p. 191

[134] Encyclopedia Britannica 2021 Online, George Gershwin, American Composer

[135] Eric Hoffer, BrainyQuotes Online

[136] Arthur Koestler, The Act of Creation, p. 211

[137] Hans Selye, M.D., The Stress of Life, (New York: McGraw Hill, 1978) p. 1

[138] Ibid, 408-409

[139] Matthew A. Stults-Kolehmainen and Rajita Sinha, The Effects of Stress on Physical Activity and Exercise, Sports Med. 2014 Jan; 44(1): 81–121

[140] Robert Keith Wallace, Ph.D., Neurophysiology of Enlightenment, p. 158-159

[141] Anastasia Toufexis, Drowsy America, Time, December 17, 1990, p. 78

[142] Stanley Coren, Dream On, The Boston Sunday Globe, August 2nd, 1998, Section C

[143] Stanley Coren, Dream On, The Boston Sunday Globe, August 2nd, 1998, Section C

[144] Anastasia Toufex, Drowsy America, p. 78-79

[145] MedicineNet, Fetus to Mom: You're Stressing Me Out, WebMD Feature

[146] WebMD, Fetus to Mom: You're Stressing Me Out

[147] Grow by WebMD, Fetus to Mom: You're Stressing Me Out

[148] Zero to Three: Birth to 12 Months, Social-Emotional Development

[149] First5LA Ages and Stages: Stress—and Stress Reduction from the Start

[150] Arthur Koestler, The Act of Creation, p. 211

[151] Jay Marcus, Success from Within, (Fairfield, Iowa: Maharishi International University Press) p. 29

[152] Ibid, p. 28

[153] Sarah DiGuilio, How What You Eat Effects your Sleep, NBC NEWS "Better," October 19, 2017

[154] Mike Adams, Good Shepherd Health Care System Online, Nutrition Counseling

[155] https://www.who.int/initiatives/behealthy/healthy-diet

[156] Matthew A. Stults-Kolehmainen and Rajita Sinha, The Effects of Stress on Physical Activity and Exercise, Sports Med. 2014 Jan; 44(1): 81–121

[157] Exercising for Better Sleep, John Hopkins Health Internet Magazine

[158] Arielle Tschinkel, 9 Signs Your Workout Is Actually Hurting You, According to Experts, Insider Internet Magazine, Jan. 11, 2021

[159] Lynch, David, Catching the Big Fish, (Tracher/Penguin 2006), p. 28

[160] Fisher, Christoper, PhD, A New EEG Study Finds That Transcendental Meditation Activates The Default Mode Network Of The Brain, bmedreports.com, March 5th, 2010

[161] Robert Keith wallace, Ph.D., The Neurophysiology of Enlightenment, p. 58

[162] Robert Keith Wallace, Ph.D. The Neurophysiology of Enlightenment, p. 121-122

[163] Robert Keith Wallace, Ph.D., The Neurophysiology of Enlightenment, (Fairfield, Iowa: Maharishi International University, 1991) p. 93-94

[164] Winfree, Arthur T., The Timing of Biological Clocks, (Scientific American Library, New York, 1986), p. 21-45

[165] Stanley Coren, Dream On, The Boston Sunday Globe, Aug. 2nd, 1998, Section C

[166] Maisel, Erik, The Creativity Book, (Penguin/Putnam, New York, 2000) p. 12

[167] Hemingway, Ernest, As quoted by Erick Maisel, IBID, p. 14

[168] Askew, Ed, www.picturequotes.com

[169] Gabaldon, Diana, www.brainyquotes.com,

[170] Mozart, Wolfgang Amadeus, As quoted by Frederich Kerst, The Man and the Artist Revealed in his own Words, (Dover Publications, New York,). P. 60

[171] Salvador Dali's Bizarre Sleep Technique Increases Creativity, Walla! Jerusalem Post Online, Dec. 25, 2021,

[172] Rosenthal, Norman E. M.D., Supermind, (A Tarcher Perigree Book, 2016) p. 47

[173] tmhome.com/experiences/tom-bergeron-transcendental-meditation-dancing-stars, online Transcendental Meditation News and More

[174] Cameron Diaz, David Lynch Foundation Video Interviewed by Bob Roth,

[175] Rosenthal, Norman E. M.D., Supermind, (A Tarcher Perigree Book, 2016) p. 81

[176] Maisel, Erik, The Creativity Book, (Penguin/Putnam, New York, DATE) p. 27-28

[177] Solomon, Maynard, Mozart: A Life, (HarperCollins, New York, 1995) p. 309

[178] James Pope Hennessy, Robert Louis Stevenson, (Simon and Schuster, New York, 1974) p. 207

[179] Vincent's Final Months, Van Gogh Museum, Online

[180] Henry David Thoreau, Walden, (Yale University Press, New Haven,2006) p. 96

[181] Arthur Koestler, The Act of Creation, p. 110

[182] Lloyd Motz, The Universe—It's Beginning and End, (New York, Charles Scribner's Sons, 1975) p. 22

[183] William Makepeace Thackery, The History of Henry Esmond

[184] Bureau of Justice Statistics, 1983

[185] George Ellis, Inside Folsom Prison, (ETC Publications, 1983) p. 12

[186] Sanford Nidich, EdD; Tom O'Connor, PhD; Thomas Rutledge, PhD, Jeff Duncan; Blaze Compton, MA; Angela Sing; Randi Nidich, EdD; The Permanente Journal, 2016, Fall; 20(4):16-007

[187] Joshua Zeitz, How World War II Almost Broke American Politics,

[188] Lao Tzu, translator, Witter Bynner, The Way of Life, According to Laotzu (The John Day Company, New York, 1944) p. 48

[189] Winona Ryder, quoted from Charlie Rose Show, February 3rd, 1997 Show Number 7021

[190] Steven Meisel, The Winona Nobody Knows, Vogue Magazine, October 1999, p. 339

[191] Albert Einstein, Telegram, 24 May 1946, sent to prominent Americans (published in New York Times, 25 May 1946)

About the Author

David Ira Rottenberg is a graduate of Columbia University. He began the practice of the Transcendental Meditation technique in 1970 and became a teacher in 1972. Along with teaching TM, he has worked as a producer for LightVideo Television and written a popular series of children's books, *Gwendolyn, the Graceful Pig, Gwendolyn Goes Hollywood,* and *Gwendolyn's Nutty Nutcracker*, another children's book, *Margarita's Star*, a young adult novel, *Outside the Edges*, a poetry book, *Soldiers of Beauty*, and co-authored three business books. He has written for publications such as Boston Magazine and the Boston Globe. His poems have appeared in poetry magazines throughout the United States. He lives in Boston, Massachusetts.